CELTC

HOW THE LEAGUE WAS WON 49 TIMES

First published 2018 by DB Publishing, an imprint of JMD Media Ltd,
Nottingham, United Kingdom.

ISBN 978-1-78091-574-6

Printed in the UK

CELTIC

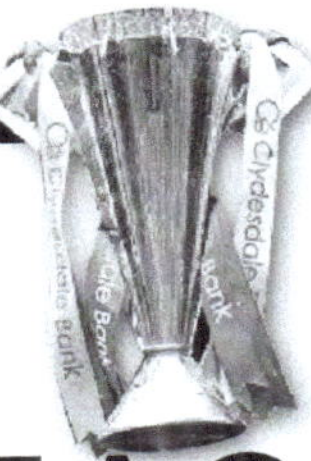

HOW THE LEAGUE WAS WON 49 TIMES

DAVID POTTER

TABLE OF CONTENTS

INTRODUCTION

Celtic have, in summer 2018, won the Scottish League (call it the Scottish Premier League, if you will) 49 times. Rangers have won it 54 times, or to be more strictly accurate, 53½ times, for in 1891 the Scottish League was shared by Rangers and Dumbarton. No one else comes near. Hibs, Aberdeen and Hearts have won it four times, next comes Dumbarton with one-and-a-half, and then five teams – Third Lanark in 1904, Motherwell in 1932, Dundee in 1962, Kilmarnock in 1965 and Dundee United on 1983 – have had their one and only, albeit spectacular, moment of glory.

So why do Celtic still lag behind Rangers? The answer to this lies in the awful years between 1938 and 1966 when Celtic won the Scottish League only once, in 1954 – and were never really close on any other occasion in these years, except perhaps when they came second to Aberdeen in 1955. Celtic had lost out most of the time to Rangers in the 1930s, had more or less gone into eclipse in the 1940s, and the 1950s had seen isolated but spectacular triumphs in other trophies, but no sustained challenge for the Scottish League apart from 1954. By the early 1960s, there was almost the belief that Celtic were not allowed to win the League and that Rangers were preordained to rule – such had been the pusillanimous approach from the Celtic Board and the relentless pro-Rangers propaganda from BBC TV and the *Scottish Daily Express* in particular.

It is often said, once famously by Billy McNeill, that in the English Civil War, Celtic would have sided with the Cavaliers rather than the Roundheads. Leaving aside any possible religious significance of that remark, what was meant was that Celtic have always been inclined to play attacking, entertaining football (and that is why they have won the European Cup and are far ahead of any other team in Scottish Cup victories) but this is not necessarily what is required to win the Scottish League. What is required more often is that ability to grind out 1–0 victories over teams like Kilmarnock and Falkirk on cold, dark, wintry days on hard pitches or boggy pitches in November and February. It must be said that Rangers have tended to do this better than Celtic. But, things are changing, aren't they?

This is not to say that Celtic have not had a great deal to be happy about in the Scottish League. Six in a row from 1905 until 1910, nine in a row from 1966 until 1974, seven in a row from 2012 until 2018 – and counting! – speak for themselves, and there have been some classic moments in those years. This book will tell the epic stories of 1909, 1915, 1968, 1979, 1986, 1998 and 2008 – all of them classic stories in their own right, but there were also the dreadful disappointments of 2003, 2005 and, to a lesser extent, 2009.

The writer remains a great believer in the psychological aspect of football. A good manager can not only make his one team win; he can make his rivals lose, even when they are playing someone else! Celtic teams must from now on take the field, confident that they are going to win and so full of self-assurance (but not arrogance or conceit) that they are going to deliver the goods to the fans who deserve so much.

"Taking their eye off the ball" is a phrase much used. It really ought not to happen. The imminence of a big game in another competition ought not to affect an apparently mundane looking League match. But the evidence suggests that it does. Celtic must always be aware of this. There is the horrendous example of 2003 when Celtic had one of their best ever seasons – yet won nothing!

We hear an awful lot of the phrase "ten in a row". It is to be encouraged.

David Potter, Kirkcaldy, June 2018.

ACKNOWLEDGEMENTS

Such a wide amount of detail has been written about Celtic that there is seldom any problem tracing any result. In recent years The Celtic Wikipedia has been a tremendous source of material and I am grateful for their input. Thanks, too, to Eric McOwat for his photographs, and for the many Celtic supporters of all ages whose brains I have picked now and again (sometimes without them being aware that I have done so) for their memories. Newspapers have also been a fertile source – *The Glasgow Herald*, *The Evening Times*, *The Dundee Courier*, *The Scotsman*, *The Aberdeen Press and Journal*, *The Daily Record* and *The Glasgow Observer* have all been consulted. To them all, I say, many thanks.

CHAPTER 1

THE FIRST TIME

1892/93

Celtic's first capture of the Scottish League took place in 1893. This was not the season-defining event that it would become in later years, for the Scottish League was a very new concept in 1893. The Scottish League was in only its third year of existence – it had been shared by Dumbarton and Rangers in 1891, and won outright by Dumbarton in 1892 – and it was struggling to gain any sort of prestige, lagging way behind the Scottish Cup which had of course started in 1874, and which Celtic had won so gloriously in 1892.

The idea of teams playing each other for points was a new one. The idea had started in England in 1889 (largely through the influence of some dynamic Scotsmen) and it had been deemed so revolutionary when it came to Scotland that Queen's Park, the oldest and most influential of Scottish clubs stayed well away from it, their lofty disdain of the idea stemming from their not entirely unjustified fear that a "League" was another step along the road to professionalism, something that caused frissons of horror among the Glasgow middle classes.

But it was a losing battle in any case, as far as Queen's Park were concerned. Professionalism was legalised in England in 1885 and widely practised in Scotland (pound notes or coins in the players shoes at the end of the game being the normal method of handing over the money!), and it was no accident that professionalism was officially recognised in Scotland more or less exactly at the time that Celtic won their first Scottish League! That John H. McLaughlin of Celtic proposed the motion legalising professionalism, added to the fact that Celtic now had a new massive stadium built to house Scotland v. England matches, was a clear indication that the days of Queen's Park running Scottish football were passing.

On the field, the Scottish Cup Finals of 1892 and 1893 had been contested by Celtic and Queen's Park. Celtic had won in 1892, but had lost narrowly in 1893 on 11 March, complaining bitterly about rough tactics from Queen's Park and also a disputed goal which Queen's Park players had convinced the referee, a Mr Harrison from Kilmarnock, was legal, whereas Celtic said the ball had gone past the post. (This was the catalyst for the introduction of goal nets.)

So there was no Scottish Cup for Celtic that year, and they had also lost the Glasgow Cup Final to Rangers, but there was the Scottish League. The Scottish League in 1893 contained only 10 teams – four from Glasgow (Celtic, Rangers, Clyde and Third Lanark), two from Edinburgh (Hearts and Leith Athletic), two from Paisley (St Mirren and Abercorn), Dumbarton and Renton. They played each other home and away but their fixtures tended to come "low down the pecking order" as it were, being played only on Saturdays when there were no Scottish

Sandy McMahon and Johnny Campbell

Cup games, Glasgow Cup games or Internationals.

This was Celtic's first season at the new Celtic Park, the envy of all Scotland, so much so that Celtic compelled both Rangers and Queen's Park to try to outdo them in future years. They reached the New Year unbeaten at Celtic Park in the Scottish League, and indeed, apart from a bad defeat at Tynecastle on 27 August and a draw at Ibrox in September, the form was really quite good. Hearts, for example, were hammered 5–0 at Celtic Park with Johnny Campbell scoring twice – it was revenge for the Tynecastle reverse – before a crowd of 10,000, a huge crowd for a domestic game at the time.

There were some superb players on show at Celtic Park. There was, for example, left-back Dan Doyle, a wild character and an unashamed professional (even before it had been legalised) and a marvellous half-back line of Maley, Kelly and Dunbar (all three of whom would play their part – in the case of Maley, a massive part – in the future development of the club) before we come to the forwards and recognise the mighty Sandy McMahon, the prince of goalscorers, dribblers and any other football attribute, a man who was well versed in the literature of Burns and Shakespeare in his spare time.

In 1893, Gladstone was Prime Minister, and as long as he was around, there was always some kind of a hope that there might one day be Home Rule for Ireland. The obstacle was of course the House of Lords, and they would block it again as they had done in 1886. It was, however, a potent issue for Celtic and their followers in the Irish community of the west of Scotland whose numbers seemed to increase every year. Scotland was industrialised and offered jobs. Ireland was agricultural with the constant fear of another famine, so Scotland, even with its obvious problems of poor housing, had clear attractions for the Irish who continued to flood in. They found their rallying and focal point in their football team.

The League had gone into a sort of hibernation over the winter months with all the Cup commitments, not to mention a few games postponed because of bad weather, but things resumed on 18 March with a 5–1 win over Dumbarton at Celtic Park. There followed away victories over Renton and Third Lanark (McMahon scoring a hat-trick in the 6–0 defeat of the Cathkin side) and then came the decisive victory over Rangers on 29 April.

It was a nice, bright but breezy day at Celtic Park with about 14,000 present. Rangers had a big support with them but it is important to realise that the great rivalry had not yet developed. Rangers represented the west of Glasgow and attracted men from the shipyards, but there was as yet nothing sectarian about them. Football was far more important than religion! Yet, even at this early stage we find Celtic frequently referred to in newspapers as "the Irishmen" and it was perhaps only natural that the supporters of the only team big enough to challenge them would begin to look on themselves as "the Scotsmen".

Celtic won the toss and played with the westerly wind behind them. They were two goals up at half-time, their goals coming from fierce shots from a distance from James Kelly and Johnny Campbell. Rangers supporters might have expected a revival in the second half when they had the benefit of the wind, but Celtic played the ball around sensibly and scored a third point near the end through Sandy McMahon.

This result left the Rangers "downcast", according to the press, and more or less won the Scottish League for Celtic. They were still, however, behind for they had 25 points from 14 games, whereas Rangers, who had played 17 games, had 26 points. (Eighteen games to be played and two points for a win.) But three of Celtic's remaining games were at home against St Mirren, Leith Athletic and Third Lanark, and the other game was at Clyde.

On Tuesday, 2 May 1893, Celtic on a heavy ground after much rain beat St Mirren (who would finish third) 4–1 with two goals each for Sandy McMahon and Johnny Campbell. It was on that very night at the meeting of the SFA that professionalism was legalised, and then in far better conditions at Barrowfield Park on Saturday, 6 May, Celtic beat Clyde 2–1 with another goal from McMahon and one from the fast improving Jimmy Blessington. Clyde had in fact scored first and were 1–0 up at half-time, but the green and white vertical stripes took control in the second half, particularly after McMahon's header. Rumours spread that Celtic had in fact won the League because Rangers had lost to Hearts at Ibrox, but such rumours proved unfounded.

Celebrations were only delayed, however, until Tuesday night at Parkhead, if "celebrations" are the right word. The crowd was poor, given as 5,000 and both *The Scotsman* and the *Glasgow Herald* fail to mention that Celtic had now won the Scottish League! However, they certainly had with two goals from Jimmy Davidson (playing against his old club) and one from Johnny Madden beating Leith Athletic 3–1.

Celtic would then go on to add the Glasgow Charity Cup to their collection, and although the disappointment of losing the Scottish Cup would stay around for some considerable time, the Scottish League was some sort of a recompense. It was the first, and the first time is always important. Other trophies won that year were:

Scottish Cup Final		
Queen's Park 2 Celtic 1	Ibrox	11 March
English Cup Final		
Wolves 1 Everton 0	Fallowfield	25 March
English League		
Sunderland		

CHAPTER 2

CHAMPIONS AGAIN

1893/94

Having won the Scottish League for the first time in 1893, Celtic repeated their success in 1894. It was in fact a repetition of 1893, in that they won the Scottish League and the Glasgow Charity Cup but lost the other two competitions. It was also the season in which, ominously for Celtic, a Glasgow team other than Queen's Park rose and challenged. This was, of course, Rangers who in 1894 after 20 years of existence won the Scottish Cup for the first time.

The Scottish League had now expanded to include a Second Division. The number of teams in the First Division, however, remained at ten, which gave 18 League fixtures, then considered the optimum for the Division. The Scottish League this year included Dundee for the first time. The efficiency of the railway system now meant that it was possible to travel to Dundee and back in a day to see a game, and for many years the Dundee game was much looked forward to by Celtic supporters as "the big day oot", with wives coming along as well to admire the new Tay Bridge opened in 1887 to replace the old one which had collapsed in the disaster of 1879. It also allowed the people in Dundee, especially the massive Irish population, a chance to see the famous team from Glasgow that was revolutionising the game.

The season opened with a 5–0 defeat of Third Lanark at Celtic Park on 12

An excellent view of a game in progress at Celtic Park in 1894. This is taken from where the Main Stand is now and is looking towards the North West.

August, then Celtic went to Dundee to play for the first time in a competitive fixture at West Craigie Park on 19 August 1893 in heatwave conditions, and the *Dundee Courier* began its lifelong love affair with Celtic by talking about a "monstra" (sic) gate of 9,000 and singing the praises of the Celtic team "cool, calculating and trained to almost everything". Celtic won 4–1 with two from Sandy McMahon, one from Joe Cassidy and a "scrimmage" which resulted in an own goal.

The inclusion of Dundee was also a welcome indication that football was expanding and that the word "Scottish" had to mean just that, not the "central belt". Aberdeen would join about a decade later, but it would be another 100 years before Inverness was included! The stress on the word "Scottish" meant that the League was now slowly gaining in prestige, although still a long way short of the Scottish Cup. Queen's Park still stayed outside the Scottish League, even though overtures were made to them. In addition, their friends in the press, notably the *Glasgow Herald*, kept saying that it would make sense for them to swallow their pride, but they would hold out for some time yet.

Celtic then drew a tight game 0–0 with Dumbarton at the end of August. But the first indication that Rangers were going to be a challenge to Celtic this year came as early as 2 September 1893. It was a very dark day in the history of the early Celts when, before a crowd of about 15,000, they went down 0–5 to Rangers at Ibrox, by some distance their biggest beating in an important game. Admittedly Willie Maley and Sandy McMahon were both out ("Celtic missed McMahon very much" says the *Glasgow Herald)* but it was simply one of those days in which Celtic had to hold up their hands and admit that Rangers were better.

Rangers would also beat Celtic in the Glasgow Cup in November – this time by

An interesting image of Dan Doyle. A "clinker" is a Victorian word for a good player.

the narrower score of 1–0 – but apart from that, Celtic's League form was splendid with particularly fine victories over Hearts at Tynecastle the week after the Ibrox debacle, and a game on 14 October against the strong-going St Bernard's, whom Celtic beat 5–2 with a Sandy McMahon hat-trick. At right-half that day, Celtic had a player called Willie Montgomery. This was no less a man than Willie Maley, who had chosen to play under his mother's maiden name for fear that his employers (Maley was only a part-time professional) might disapprove of him playing professional football!

There was also an excellent game of football a couple of days before Christmas at Dumbarton when they won 5–4. "Without an inch of dubiety" about 8,000 were at Boghead that midwinter's day and they saw a great game that finished in "crepuscular penumbra" (even though half-time had been little more than a turnaround). At one point late in the second half, Dumbarton were 3–2 up but a flurry of late goals saw Celtic equalise to make it 4–4 until, with literally the last kick of the ball, Sandy McMahon scored the winner.

Even better news came Celtic's way that day when the "tidings" came through that Third Lanark had beaten Rangers at Ibrox 3–0. "The play of their much thought-of backs was simply wretched" says the *Dundee Courier* and this result meant that Celtic were now clear at the top with only six games left to be played. Celtic then finished the calendar year of 1893 with a fine 3–1 win over Third Lanark at Cathkin, with goals from John Divers, Jimmy Blessington and inevitably Sandy McMahon.

In the event, the Scottish Cup and the Scottish League were decided on two consecutive Saturdays in February. Celtic had in January beaten St Bernard's 2–1 at Logie Green in Edinburgh, and then St Mirren 5–1 at Celtic Park on 10 February in an excellent display of "brisk" football in the wind and the sleet. The Scottish League was thus almost won (Rangers had dropped another point to St Mirren in late January) by the time that Rangers came to Celtic Park on 24 February.

This game, however, can only be seen in the context of what happened the week before when the two teams met at Hampden to contest the Scottish Cup Final, a game which sadly went the way of Rangers, who won their first ever Scottish Cup by beating Celtic 3–1. Maley played although ill and at a key point to the game, Johnny Campbell picked up a cross from McMahon and blazed over the bar. Rangers took hold of the game in the second half, scored three times and Maley's consolation goal was of little comfort to Celtic. The game was played in awful conditions before 17,000 at Hampden.

This was clearly a major disappointment for the team, but the chance for revenge came next week. Not everyone would agree with the assessment of the *Dundee Courier* that the Scottish League was "infantile" in comparison with the Scottish Cup, but it was certainly second best, as was evidenced by the crowd which numbered about 10,000, a good deal down on last week's attendance. The weather conditions were similar, and Celtic approached this game with a grim determination that Rangers must not be allowed to defeat them four times this season. This time Maley did not play and Campbell was also out, but their places were filled more than adequately by Charlie McEleny and John Divers.

The game was tough with a certain evidence that some of the happenings of last week were being carried on to this week, but this time it was Celtic who triumphed. Celtic scored through McMahon and Blessington, and then after Rangers had equalised, Joe Cassidy scored the winner. It is odd to find the Scottish League described as a "consolation" but this was the way that late Victorian football was. However, Celtic had now won "the flag" for the second year in a row. They would go on to lose their last two League games to Hearts (Hearts finished second that season) and Leith Athletic, but no one seemed to be too concerned about that, and in any case, there was a further honour gained when Celtic won the Glasgow Charity Cup to make it a successful season once again.

Scottish Cup Final		
Rangers 3 Celtic 1	Hampden	17 February
English Cup Final		
Notts County 4 Bolton 1	Goodison	31 March
English League		
Aston Villa		

CHAPTER 3

TRIUMPHANT AGAIN

1895/96

Celtic won their third Scottish League title in season 1895/96. It was a remarkable campaign won with a tremendous degree of panache and style, and was all wrapped up well before the turn of the year. This was the idea in those days, so that after New Year, clubs could turn to what was considered the more important trophy, namely the Scottish Cup. Celtic would not win the Scottish Cup in 1896 in what could justly be considered to be unfair circumstances, but the months from August to December 1895 could well be considered to be among the more remarkable of the club's history. Not only did they win the ten-team Scottish League First Division, they also created their record victory, sustained their record home defeat and won the Glasgow Cup into the bargain!

1895 had not been a great season for Celtic. St Bernard's had won the Scottish Cup, Hearts had won the Scottish League (it was indeed a great time for Edinburgh because Hibernian won the Second Division) and Celtic, riven by internal discord – a common theme in the early days and one which would get a lot worse in 1897 – were nowhere.

Celtic began the season without Johnny Campbell, who had gone to Aston Villa. Willie Maley talks vaguely about the "stupid action" of a "very prominent committee man" causing the departure of the talented Campbell. Campbell would win the English League with Villa in 1896 and the League and Cup Double in 1897. His replacement was a man called Allan Martin from Hibs and he would have a good season. But there was still Sandy McMahon, now commonly referred to as "the Duke".

The season started in sweltering heat at Carolina Port, the new enclosure of Dundee FC, and Celtic delighted the 10,000 crowd with a 2–1 win, the goals coming from Martin and McMahon. Two weeks later came the first reverse as they went to Easter Road to play the newly promoted Hibernian and they lost 4–2, to the delight of a nasty Hibs crowd who barracked the Celtic players. They could hardly have called then "Fenian" or "Papist" as the supporters of other clubs like St Mirren and Hearts did, but there was a resentment of the success of the Glasgow Irishmen who were accused (not without cause) of having robbed Hibs of some of their star players like Sandy McMahon and Willie Groves a few years ago. Jealousy of Celtic is sadly a common theme in Hibs circles.

This was a blow to Celtic but they then went on a tour of England in early September. Results were bad and behaviour was worse, with even the normally cool-headed Sandy McMahon being involved in some off the field "incidents". When they came back to play their game at Ibrox on 7 September, we find that

McMahon and Doyle were out of the side, whether suspended, injured or just simply "dropped" we do not know. Surprisingly, however, the Celtic side played well and before 15,000 defeated Rangers 4–2 on a very windy day at Ibrox.

The two miscreants were still missing for the next game, the home fixture against Hearts, but this time the result was a great deal less happy, for Celtic went down 0–5 to Hearts who spotted all the weaknesses in the Celtic line up and inflicted on Celtic their record home defeat. 18,000 were there – a huge crowd for the time – and Celtic were simply "overmatched" as *The Scotsman* put it. Only James Kelly earned any kind of plaudits from the crowd, the rest of the team being subject to a certain amount of "hissing" and some of the crowd even beginning to applaud the excellence of the men from Edinburgh who had brought with them a huge support of over 1,000, to the delight of the railway companies.

Two days later, on the Monday, it being the Edinburgh holiday weekend, Celtic travelled to the capital to play St Bernard's at Logie Green. McMahon was restored for that game, but the team performance was little better, for Celtic lost again 0–3 and left Edinburgh trying to claim that it was all the referee's fault.

Anyone who suggested at this point that Celtic were likely to become League Champions might have been deemed a candidate for "bedlam" (as they called mental hospitals in the Victorian age) but after that, Celtic rallied. Dan Doyle came back, clearly determined to behave and to set an example, and after a tight

Sandy McMahon has the ball at his feet and Willie Maley is on the extreme right at the front row.

couple of games against Dumbarton at Boghead and Hibs at Celtic Park, the goals began to flow.

At the end of October, Celtic defeated Dundee 11–0 at Celtic Park. Everything about this game was "farcical" as Willie Maley put it. The conditions were poor after some overnight snow and sleet, Dundee were racked with internal fighting, some of their men got injured on the wet pitch and Celtic took full advantage – so full that no two sources are in agreement about who actually scored all the goals! It could indeed have been a lot more.

And then we come to November 1895, possibly the best month in the club's history to date. On 9 November, Third Lanark were thrashed 7–0 to the delight of the fans, on the 16th the Glasgow Cup was won at Ibrox when Celtic beat Queen's Park 6–3, and then on the 23rd the team travelled to Edinburgh to play Hearts in the return League fixture. Here revenge was dished out with 15,000 (including a large contingent form Glasgow who escorted their players to and from the ground lest they be attacked by Edinburgh "ruffians") witnessing an emphatic 4–1 win with goals from McMahon, Blessington and two from Martin.

Celtic were now back in the League race, particularly when they heard that Rangers had beaten Hibs 4–0 (this was a good result for Celtic, for Rangers had started the campaign even worse than Celtic had and were only outside candidates for the League flag) and the next two games against the Saints (the western Saints of St Mirren and the eastern ones of St Bernard's) were both hard fought victories, the game at Paisley on 30 November being as good an example of Celtic's fighting spirit as one is likely to see. Goalless at half-time, St Mirren then opened the scoring early in the second half, before Jimmy Blessington scored twice and then Willie Ferguson scrambling a late clincher in a game that was not bereft of incidents on and off the park.

Celtic's defeat of St Bernard's at Parkhead on 7 December was even tighter but the goals scored by McMahon and Martin (as well as results elsewhere) meant that Celtic were now in a position to win the Scottish League if they won their next fixture. Their opponents? Rangers. Most unusually for the times, newspaper space was devoted to the "build up" to the game with things being said like "only a Scotland–England game could grip Glasgow like this", and a huge crowd of 24,000 made their way to Celtic Park to see this encounter. The weather was appalling (it was 14 December) with heavy rain, otherwise who knows what the attendance might have been? As it was, 24,000 was huge for Victorian Britain.

The weather began to abate a little with showers rather than persistent rain, but the ground was still heavy. Not that it bothered Celtic, for the green and white verticals dominated the game and won easily 6–2. Martin scored twice as did McMahon and Blessington and Battles scored the other two. "Towards the end Celtic did pretty much as they liked" to the delight of the huge crowd who had paid £707 (almost inconceivable for Victorian Scotland) for the privilege. This triggered off party time in the East End, with scenes reminiscent of 1892 when they won the Scottish Cup. The League had been in existence for six years, and Celtic had won it three times. "Home Rule for Ireland would not have been nicer" said a committee man.

1896 thus dawned with Celtic the champions and favourites to win the Scottish Cup. Sadly they went out in the First Round to Queen's Park, but Celtic cried "foul" claiming that Queen's Park had used their influence to set the date for Barney Battles' disciplinary hearing and ensuring his suspension for the game. Not that it really helped Queen's Park, for Hearts won the Scottish Cup.

Scottish Cup Final		
Hearts 3 Hibernian 1	Logie Green	14 March
English Cup Final		
The Wednesday 2 Wolves 1	Crystal Palace	18 April
English League		
Sunderland		

CHAPTER FOUR

MALEY'S FIRST LEAGUE TITLE

1897/98

Sometimes in football, as in life, a disaster is the necessary catalyst for something good to happen. As far as Celtic were concerned, the year 1897 typified that. Fourth in the Scottish League was bad enough but it was the Scottish Cup defeat at Arthurlie in January 1897 which highlighted the problems and difficulties, if not the actual impossibility of an amateurish committee structure running a massive organisation like Celtic had become.

To the credit of those who were running the club, things changed fairly quickly behind the scenes, and on the actual playing side of the club a major and significant step was made in the appointment of Willie Maley, one-time player and later committee member, to be the "Match Secretary". It was not quite the post of "manager" as we know it in the modern sense of the word, but such was the strength of character of Willie Maley and his passionate love for the green and white that he very soon took over the running of the playing side of the club. He was indeed "the man who made Celtic".

Maley's first season in charge of the club (although no one at the time would use the phrase "in charge of", for Maley was now technically an employee) was a great success as Celtic once again won the Scottish League for the fourth time out of eight years. He was fortunate with injuries, in that Sandy McMahon played for most of the season, and Maley was also able to entice back to Celtic Park from Aston Villa the great Johnny Campbell, the friend and colleague of McMahon. Campbell had been phenomenally successful in England, playing his part in Aston Villa's winning of the English League and Cup double in 1897, but he was a Glasgow boy at heart, loved the Celtic and was one of the first to say that "the first result I look for in the evening paper is that of Celtic". When invited back, he came like a shot.

Another significant acquisition was that of James Welford, who had played alongside Campbell at Aston Villa. He was an English county cricket player for Warwickshire as well, and became a sturdy right-back to partner Dan Doyle. Maley also acquired the services of George "Dod" Allan from Liverpool, a fast running forward who enjoyed Celtic's famous "passing game", but there was one addition that he, for the moment, stopped short of. This was Barney Battles, a man who had disgraced himself by being involved in the "strike" of 1896 and had been moved on to Liverpool. He was less than totally happy there, however, and made it plain that he was sorry for his "subversive activities" and would love to return to play for the club that he loved, especially as he had a total respect for Willie Maley. His day would come, but not yet. In the meantime he returned to Scotland to play

Barney Battles in the Rosebery colours of Scotland.

for Dundee where, as we shall see, he played a significant part for Celtic this season.

The League season opened in fine style and in fine weather at Celtic Park, with a 4–1 win over Hibernian. The crowd was given as 12,000 and even without McMahon, Celtic won comfortably. Last season's champions Hearts then held them to a 0–0 draw at Tynecastle, but four successive victories followed, the most significant being a 4–0 win at Ibrox on the Holiday Monday of 27 September.

A huge crowd of 31,000 in glorious weather packed the somewhat primitive Ibrox Stadium and there were a few minor injuries caused by crushing, and at one point an encroachment onto the field by youngsters who feared that they were about to be injured "as the crowd swayed to and fro". The press is at pains to stress, however, that the crowd was well behaved and that there were "no fisticuffs" even though a few individuals had to be escorted from the scene "to reflect on the wisdom or otherwise, of having celebrated their Holiday Monday too exuberantly".

It was a game which Celtic simply took control of, the four goals being scored by four separate players – McMahon, King, Campbell and Allan – and the crowd being noisily appreciative of the good football on view. Campbell was quoted in the *Daily Record* as saying that he was as proud of that performance as he was of his English Cup medal with Aston Villa last year. Allan was badly injured by a crude tackle from Drummond of Rangers – "a most regrettable incident" as the *Glasgow Herald* states it with a hint of meiosis – but Celtic finished the game well on top and Rangers were demoralised.

A few weeks later on 23 October in an even more significant result, Celtic beat Hearts 3–2 at Celtic Park. A late headed goal from Campbell from an Alec King cross gave Celtic a victory in a very entertaining game which thrilled the 16,000 crowd, but the *Glasgow Herald* also praises the efforts of Hearts who "gave McArthur no end of bother" – but the diminutive Dan was up to the demands of the day, diving time and time again at the feet of Hearts forwards and "punching clear" on many occasions.

Two weeks later at Carolina Port on 6 November 1897, it was the lesser known Adam Henderson (in for the once again injured McMahon) who won the day for Celtic with two fine goals to delight the large crowd, but then Celtic became embroiled in a prolonged Glasgow Cup battle with Rangers which took three games to resolve and which Celtic eventually lost. But this team bounced back from that and in the five weeks from late November until the New Year recorded five victories and finished the year unbeaten in the Scottish League. Christmas Day saw a 9–1 hammering of Clyde at Barrowfield Park with George Allan netting (if they had goal nets at Barrowfield Park) no fewer than five goals.

The New Year's Day game at Celtic Park against Rangers had to be abandoned because of repeated crowd encroachment – such was the passionate interest in the game in Glasgow – but Celtic then beat Dundee and Partick Thistle to put themselves within touching distance of the League flag, the only fly in the ointment being a heartbreaking Scottish Cup defeat to Third Lanark, after last year's nemesis Arthurlie had been disposed of.

The League was won with a game to spare on 12 February when Celtic beat St Mirren rather easily in the rain at Parkhead with two goals from Pat Gilhooly and one from Davie Russell. That itself was not enough to win the League that day, but a telegram from Dundee confirmed that Celtic were the champions. Dundee had beaten Rangers 2–1 and Barney Battles, "a glutton for work" according to the *Dundee Courier*, had scored one of the goals! This meant that Rangers could not now mathematically catch Celtic even if they were to win the replayed game from New Year. It also meant that more and more pressure was being piled on Celtic to take back Barney Battles "once a Celt, always a Celt" whom the *Glasgow Observer*, unashamedly pro-Celtic as ever, describes as "St Bernard Battles, Patron of Parkhead".

The triumph was a significant one for Celtic in that it proved that last year was a one-off disaster and that no permanent damage had been done to the club, which had been in existence for only a decade, yet had made such a huge difference to the cultural life of those who loved it and to the Scottish scene in general. But this League triumph would be the last for some considerable time, for it was now the turn of the other Glasgow team with a large support. They played in the west of the city and their supporters worked in the shipyards. Their supporters (and their families) tended to be the victims not so much of the Irish Potato Famine, but of the equally shameful and tragic Highland Clearances.

Scottish Cup Final		
Rangers 2 Kilmarnock 0	Hampden	26 March
English Cup Final		
Nottingham Forest 3 Derby County 1	Crystal Palace	16 April
English League		
Sheffield United		

CHAPTER 5

"HERE WE GO, SIX IN A ROW"

1904/05

Willie Maley's new and young Celtic side "arrived" on 16 April 1904 in that never to be forgotten Scottish Cup Final against Rangers which featured Jimmy Quinn's epic hat-trick. That was a great day for the club, its main significance being in that it acted as a springboard for what was to come. The Cup was all about glory; the League was about graft and consistency, but people were beginning more and more to realise that the winner of the Scottish League was undeniably the best team in Scotland.

Since Celtic's winning of the League in 1898, performances had been disappointing. Rangers had won the League four times in a row and then Hibs and Third Lanark had a year each, but Celtic were, to a certain extent at least, in the doldrums. But work was going on behind the scenes at a phenomenal rate, as Maley began to build his young team, recruiting men like Jimmy McMenemy from Rutherglen Glencairn, Jimmy Quinn from Croy and possibly as important as any, Jimmy Young (soon to be called "Sunny") a Kilmarnock boy now homesick playing for Bristol Rovers.

Celtic's mighty half-back line of Young, Loney and Hay.

Summer 1904 was spent like summer 1965 was. A Scottish Cup after a few years of lack of success was a tremendous impetus and stimulus for the support as they anticipated great things to come. They would not be entirely disappointed, but it would not be all plain sailing either, at least in the early days. The enthusiasm for the new season was by no means diminished by the fire at Celtic Park in May, which destroyed the old grandstand on the north side of the ground.

Since Celtic's previous success in 1898, the Scottish League First Division had now expanded to 14 teams and therefore 26 games were played. The Scottish League had successfully recruited the hitherto somewhat snobby Queen's Park to condescend and join the professional League, while they themselves remains strictly amateur, and possibly as a result, the League had now gained a little in prestige, even though for a long time after this the Scottish Cup would retain its superiority and priority in fixture arranging, for example.

The only team who seriously troubled Celtic in the first half of the 1904/05 season was Hearts. They drew at Parkhead, and then on the Edinburgh Holiday Monday at Tynecastle, Hearts beat Celtic 2–0. The cause of this defeat was "miserable shooting" on the part of the Celtic forwards, although most newspapers agreed that Celtic were the better side.

Celtic bounced back from this, and after an important success in beating Rangers to win the Glasgow Cup in early October, drew with them the following week in the League at Celtic Park. Further draws came against Hibs, Queen's Park and Partick Thistle, but apart from that, Celtic slowly developed into a cohesive unit winning games (not always spectacularly) but with discerning spectators noting that the half-back line of Young, Loney and Hay was beginning to "take a hold of games".

Celtic's good 3–1 win over Kilmarnock at Celtic Park on Hogmanay ensured that the team finished 1904 at the top of the League four points ahead of Rangers but with an extra game played. But then things began to wobble a little bit. The fixture at Ibrox on 2 January was lost to bad weather, and then the following day Celtic disappointed their fans by going down 2–3 at home to Airdrie, it being no coincidence that the half-back line of Young, Loney and Hay was disrupted that day as Hay had to play at left-back because of an injury to Willie Orr and a youngster called Eck McNair was hideously out of position at left-half.

A further disaster followed on 14 January at Dens Park, Dundee. On a hard and slippery pitch the home side won 2–1, with Peter Somers' opportunist goal not enough to win the day for Celtic. This meant that with Celtic only having four games left in the League, they were two points ahead of Rangers, but Rangers had two games in hand. With the New Year's game at Ibrox still to be played, the advantage was very much with Rangers.

But Celtic kept the head well, the benefits of Maley's taking them away to Seamill Hydro now and again to breathe in the ozone (while creating a team spirit at the same time) beginning to manifest themselves. They beat Hibs 2–0 the following week, then Morton 5–2 on 4 February, and then two weeks after that came the game at Ibrox. The press is generally surprised by just how much Celtic were on top of Rangers in this game, for the teams approached this fixture equally balanced. The key factor was the strong wind. Celtic played against it in the first half and held Rangers to 1–1, but then simply tore them apart in the second half, Jimmy Quinn scoring twice and Davie Hamilton twice. Two weeks later at Motherwell, Celtic completed their League programme with a 6–2 hammering of a very poor home side, and this time Jimmy Quinn scored a hat-trick and the other goals came from Willie Loney, Peter Somers and Eck McNair.

This meant that Celtic had now completed their League form with 41 points from 26 games. The problem was that Rangers could still equal them, for their 23 games had yielded 35 points. There did not at this stage seem to be any clear idea of what would happen if both teams finished level on points. Goal average was still only a theoretical possibility, and there was a precedent of 1891 when Dumbarton and Rangers were declared joint champions. But for the moment this was set to one side while the International games and the Scottish Cup were played out.

The Scottish Cup was nasty this year. In the semi-final at Celtic Park, Jimmy Quinn was wrongly sent off and a riot ensued. This whole thing would become a "cause celebre" of Edwardian Scotland, but for the moment Celtic were compelled to concede the tie. There was no little delight at Celtic Park when Third Lanark defeated Rangers in the Scottish Cup Final, but before that happened Rangers had defeated Morton and Port Glasgow Athletic at Ibrox in the Scottish League to move within two points of Celtic.

It was as late as 29 April before Rangers finished their programme beating Morton 2–0 at Cappielow. Celtic and Rangers were thus tied at the top. Rangers would have won on goal average if that system had obtained, but no one at the Scottish League seemed to know what to do. The *Dundee Courier* describes the Scottish League as an organisation worked by "wire pulling", but on this occasion someone had a bright idea. Celtic and Rangers were due to play in 6 May in a little respected competition called the Glasgow League. Why not "double" this game as a League decider and move the game to Hampden to ensure neutrality?

This idea did indeed find favour – naturally, for it meant money and a 30,000 crowd – and thus for the first and only time in Scottish League history, we had a play-off to decide the champions. A further attempt to ensure neutrality lay in the appointment of an Englishman, Mr Kirkham from Preston, to be the referee.

The game was, as usual, all about Jimmy Quinn, but it was not he who scored the goals. But he was employed to play the role of the decoy, a job that he tackled with relish and enthusiasm, running about all over the pitch and taking at least one man with him. This game was decided in the second half within the space of a few minutes and it was Jimmy McMenemy and Davie Hamilton who did the needful. Rangers pulled one back, but it was the Celtic supporters who "were dancing on the cinders" on the terracing of the new Hampden Park. Everyone behaved, and

Scottish Cup Final		
Third Lanark 3 Rangers 1	Hampden	15 April
(after 0-0 in the first game)		
English Cup Final		
Aston Villa 2 Newcastle United 0	Crystal Palace	15 April
English League		
Newcastle United		

Celtic were presented with the League flag a few weeks later. They also added to their League success by lifting the Glasgow Charity Cup at the end of May.

This League title was their first such success in the 20th century, and a new era of Celtic dominance had begun. The team was young and talented, their manager was genial, enthusiastic and knowledgeable, and Celtic were now to change Scottish football for some considerable time.

CHAPTER 6

BUILDING A GREAT SIDE

1905/06

Having achieved the breakthrough in the Scottish League, albeit in somewhat unusual and unprecedented circumstances in a play-off in May 1905, something that was never destined to be repeated, Celtic then proceeded in season 1905/06 to consolidate and then to show the world that there was a somewhat special team at Celtic Park.

In modern terminology "there was a buzz about the place" as this young and ambitious side began to play good, entertaining football and even to win round those who were for any reason opposed to Celtic. Perhaps the greatest achievement around this time was Maley's ability to spread the gospel, as it were, and to win round people from outwith Celtic's original power base of the Glasgow Irish. True, the Glasgow Irish would remain solidly pro-Celtic – and more than 100 years later still do – but now others were happy to join them.

The increasingly broad-based nature of the club was reflected in the players. Quite a few – Jimmy Young, Jimmy Hay, Alec Bennett, Alec McNair for example – had no obvious Irish connection, yet they all loved the green and white. And the actual green and white stripe in itself was an attraction. They had moved from vertical to horizontal stripes in 1903 and it seemed no accident that that was when the team took off. Football being the psychological game that it undeniably is, the team seemed young and new, and seemed to move a lot faster in their stripes than did their opponents in solid red or blue.

Celtic's form in the autumn of 1905 was consistently good. The Glasgow Cup was won in October – always a good

Jimmy Quinn

feeling to have one trophy under your belt at an early stage of the season – and the team reached New Year with only two defeats and one draw in the Scottish League. The first division of the Scottish League had been expanded yet again so that it now included 16 clubs with the admission of Falkirk and Aberdeen. There was as yet no automatic promotion or relegation between Divisions One and Two. Clyde actually won Division Two in 1905, but Falkirk clearly "knocked on a few doors", and the claims of the large and rich city in the north-east could hardly be ignored if this was to be a genuinely "Scottish" League.

Celtic won their first three League games but then drew with Hearts at Tynecastle on the Edinburgh Holiday Monday in September and it was a thrilling affair. Hearts would have a good season – in fact, they would be Celtic's main challengers and go on to win the Scottish Cup – and they had a marvellous forward called Bobby Walker who soon earned the nickname "Houdini" after the famous escapologist of the day. This was a fine, even, sporting game much enjoyed by a 12,000 crowd.

Celtic's two reverses before the New Year were to Rangers at Ibrox in October, another great game in which a draw would have been a fairer result, and then a real shocker on 11 November to Port Glasgow Athletic at Parkhead. There were extenuating circumstances, however, in that Young and McMenemy were out, the game was played throughout in "biblical rain" before a very small crowd, and when Celtic were awarded a penalty kick early in the second half, Willie Orr had one of his rare misses.

Apart from these reverses, the form was good with not a single goal conceded in the month of December – 1–0 against Aberdeen, Hibs and Port Glasgow ("revenge is sweet" purred Mr Maley) and two 4–0 thumpings of Motherwell and Morton. The year ended at Easter Road in very pleasant weather for 30 December, and Celtic won with a last-minute goal from Jimmy Quinn who picked up a ball from McMenemy and ran through between the two Hibs full-backs to score, making the home followers "frantic with rage", according to the *Dundee Courier* while *The Scotsman*, a lover of Hearts in those days, is upset that Hearts' narrow defeat by Motherwell meant that Celtic now finished 1905 a point ahead of Hearts and with two games in hand.

40,000 were at Celtic Park for the New Year fixture against Rangers. The fine mild weather continued, and the large crowd saw a very close fixture which might have gone either way but from which Celtic emerged victorious winning 1-0 with a late drive from Davie Hamilton, only partially saved by Tommy Sinclair "but ere he could recover, the ball was past him" according to the *Glasgow Herald*.

Early 1906 saw other things dominating the news in the shape of a general election. In those days general elections took weeks, with voting going on in different parts of the country on different days. Very early on, however, it appeared that there was going to be a Liberal landslide. This was good news for the Celtic community for it promised much-needed social reform but it also meant, significantly for the Irish in Glasgow, that Home Rule for Ireland was back on the agenda. There was thus excitement in the air as Celtic marched triumphantly through January scoring goals galore: 7–0 against Falkirk, 5–2 against Airdrie and 4–1 against Partick Thistle. Such consistent form meant that by the end of January, Celtic were five points ahead of Hearts and a game in hand. With only six games to go, they began to look "uncatchable".

But February was not quite so good. Celtic had beaten Dundee in a very tight game at Dens Park in the Scottish Cup the week before, and now as luck would have it, they were back for a League fixture the following week. This time Dundee won 1–0, but as challengers Hearts and Rangers also lost on that cold day on 3 February 1906, little damage was done. For the game at Dens Park, Quinn was out injured, McMenemy had a poor game and Hamilton was brutally hacked by the Dundee full-back Henderson who was out for a little revenge from last week. It was a disappointment, however, but nothing like the disaster that came Celtic's way on 24 February in the Scottish Cup when 52,000 at Celtic Park saw Hearts put them out of the Scottish Cup. It was a major blow for Maley's young side.

But Celtic had beaten St Mirren in the League game on 17 February, and thus travelled to Pittodrie for their first ever League game at that venue knowing that a victory would win them the Scottish League. The crowd of 10,000 contained a surprising amount of Celtic supporters who travelled up on the train, taking the opportunity to see the Granite City perhaps, but the surprising thing was that the game actually went ahead when McNair, McLeod and Quinn were all playing for Scotland against Wales at Tynecastle! It turned out to be a bad day for everyone. The Black and Golds of Aberdeen beat a lacklustre Celtic side 1–0 and Scotland went down to Wales.

But for Celtic, "Paradise was only postponed, not lost" when, on the following Saturday, they went to Hampden and defeated bottom team Queen's Park 6–0. Jimmy Quinn, who seemed to have a particular fondness for Hampden Park, was totally rampant and unstoppable that day scoring four goals, Bennett and McMenemy scoring the others. 15,000 stood and "cheered themselves hoarse" at this performance, and it was one of the days when Celtic won the League in

Scottish Cup Final
Hearts 1 Third Lanark 0 — Hampden — 28 April

English Cup Final
Everton 1 Newcastle United 0 — Crystal Palace — 21 April

English League
Liverpool

style. Their final game of the League season might have been a thriller when Hearts came to Celtic Park. In fact, it was an anticlimax, won 1–0 by already-champions Celtic on the late date of 21 April with Hearts having their eye on next week's Scottish Cup Final.

Thus Celtic had won their sixth League Championship. There had been one or two reverses and disappointments, but there had also been some blistering moments of great Celtic play, mainly in the midwinter months of December and January. The team was, however, still young – a certain immaturity had cost them the Scottish Cup and the Glasgow Charity Cup – and developing. There was a great deal more to come, and things remained bright down Parkhead way.

CHAPTER 7

THE FIRST DOUBLE

1906/07

Since the inception of the Scottish League in 1890, the organisation had seen a steady increase in interest, membership and prestige. It had begun as a sort of afterthought to prevent teams playing so many friendlies, and it did provide regular fixtures, home and away. Unlike the Glasgow League, which was soon discarded, the Scottish League grew and grew and now, in summer 1906, the decision was taken to expand the League to 18 clubs in the First Division and 12 in the Second Division. The idea 10 years ago when the League was smaller had been to play League fixture until the New Year and then to concentrate on the Scottish Cup and Internationals. This was clearly impossible now.

It was frequently remarked that no team had as yet won the Scottish League and the Scottish Cup in the same year. Celtic's good teams of the 1890s had never done that and even the Rangers team of 1898/99, which had won every League game it played, had fallen to Celtic in the 1899 Scottish Cup Final. The "double" had been done in England by "proud Preston" in the very first year of the English League in 1889, and then famously by "the villains" Aston Villa of Birmingham in 1897, but it had never happened in Scotland. Willie Maley of Celtic was determined to be the first.

The season started with Celtic going off at the speed of an express train. (This being the age of the railway, track metaphors abounded in the press with Jimmy Quinn, for example, being called "the Croy express" and when an attack failed, it "hit the buffers" of the defence and so on.) They won their first 10 games (and that included the Glasgow Cup semi-final and final) before they drew with Dundee 0–0 on 20 October. It was the Glasgow Cup Final of 6 October before they lost a goal and in each of the first eight games, Jimmy Quinn scored at least once!

What made this remarkable was that there were players missing through injury. Centre-half Willie Loney injured himself against Hearts on 15 September and was out for more or less the rest of the season, and right-winger Alec Bennett was out as well, being replaced by the charismatic Bobby Templeton. Templeton was a remarkable soldier of fortune. He was a huge entertainer and was "credited" (if that is the right word) for indirectly causing the

Ibrox Disaster of 1902 at the Scotland v. England international. A long ball across the park from the right to "the Blue Streak" (as he was called) on the left meant the crowd in the wooden stand swayed as well and too much pressure was put on the wooden floorboards.

But an even more remarkable recruitment came in goal. Davie Adams, playing in a benefit match at Ibrox before the season started, injured his hand on a nail sticking out of the post. The embarrassed Rangers manager William Wilton (a close friend of Willie Maley) immediately offered Celtic the services of their reserve goalkeeper Tommy Sinclair who had now lost his place in the first team. Tommy came into the Celtic team, kept eight clean sheets and even won a Glasgow Cup medal before returning to Ibrox when Davie Adams came back. Even more remarkably, he was then moved on to Newcastle United, for whom he played a few games as they won the English League that year!

With a start like that, it was always going to be difficult to catch Celtic. In any case, the good form continued and Celtic reached the New Year undefeated and with only three draws to their discredit. Jimmy Quinn kept scoring the goals, and the absence of Loney was hardly noticed for Eck McNair filled in at centre-half. McNair would become a legend at right-back, but this season he played at centre-half. Even when Jimmy Hay was out injured as well, the absence was scarcely noticed, such was the excellence of the side with form particularly impressive in the month of December, the month where oddly enough the destination of the League is often decided.

Both Old Firm League games this year (and Celtic and Rangers were now called the "Old Firm" for their perceived capacity for making money!) were 2–1 wins for the home side, and in each case the opinion of the press is that a draw would have been a fairer result. The New Year's Day defeat at Ibrox was the first reverse of the season, but a glance at the League table showed that Celtic were comfortable at the top – four points clear of second placed Dundee with two games in hand.

But that was not the main topic of conversation that New Year. Jimmy Quinn had been sent off after intervening to remonstrate with Rangers full-back Joe Hendry after a nasty tackle on Alec Bennett. Jimmy slipped on the wet ground and charged into Hendry. Jimmy was then sent off more or less as a scapegoat for other perceived indiscretions from various players on either side, and when he was banned for two months, the Celtic support were rightly outraged. Celtic now had to do without Jimmy Quinn as well as Willie Loney!

Not that it really mattered. Another four victories followed in January, the one at Celtic Park against Morton on 19 January seeing Eck McNair in the centre-forward position and scoring! February saw a prolonged embroilment with Morton in the Scottish Cup, and the next League match was not played until 2 March at Pittodrie. Sunny Jim was playing for the Scottish

Peter Somers

League against the English League at Ibrox that day, and he was badly missed, but Davie Adams in goal had a great game in defying the "wasps" (as Aberdeen were called) and earning a draw.

Next week Jimmy Quinn "the idol of Paradise" returned. His first game was a good Scottish Cup win at Ibrox, but then a weakened team lost to Third Lanark, and the week after that, they could only earn a goalless draw against challengers Dundee at Celtic Park. At one point Dundee appeared to have the ball over the line but the goal was not given, and Celtic missed a few chances as well but the end result was that with seven games left, Celtic were still three points ahead of Dundee with a game in hand.

On the Holiday Monday of 1 April in fine spring weather, Celtic beat Queen's Park 2–1 at Celtic Park while across the city Rangers did Celtic a favour by drawing 2–2 with Dundee. The next few games involved the Scottish Cup – a glorious win for Celtic over Hearts in the final on 20 April after more of a struggle against Hibs in the semi-final – but Dundee's failure to win all their games meant that all Celtic had to do to win the Scottish League was to win one of their remaining six games.

The first of these was against Partick Thistle at Meadowside on Wednesday, 24 April. Although Celtic brought the Scottish Cup with them, hoping to persuade more people to attend, Wednesday was a working day and even with a late afternoon kick-off failed to attract any more than 4,000 to appear. It was therefore a sort of an anticlimax as Celtic comfortably beat Thistle 2–0, with the influence of Jimmy Quinn once more apparent. He set up Bennett for the first goal in the first half, then ran through to score the second in the latter stages of the game.

Celtic has thus "scaled the Scottish Everest" as a newspaper put it with the winning of both Scottish trophies in the one season. As they had also carried off the Glasgow Cup in October, they only needed the Glasgow Charity Cup for the full set. Sadly they went down 0–1 to Rangers in the final at Cathkin on 18 May. Mr Maley, apparently, was less than totally pleased, but three out of four was by no means bad. And, as the team was still developing, next year would be even better!

The other trophy winners that season were:

Scottish Cup Final		
Celtic 3 Hearts 0	Hampden	20 April
English Cup Final		
Sheffield Wednesday 2 Everton 1	Crystal Palace	20 April
English League		
Newcastle United		

CHAPTER 8

THE GREATEST SHOW ON EARTH

1907/08

This was the team of all the talents, the "greatest show on earth" (as they also said about the Barnum and Bailey circus at the same time) and until 1967 the undisputed greatest Scottish team ever. When 1967 came along, a certain amount of doubt crept into it, but if those who were fortunate enough to see both (you would have to be very young in 1908 and very old in 1967!) could not differentiate between the two of them, then we must declare it a draw and say that in the same way that the 1967 team dealt with everything that was put in front of them, so too did the heroes of 1908.

In the Scottish League, they were actually defeated three times at the difficult venues of Pittodrie, Tynecastle and Dens Park but recovered quickly. They were not without their absences or injury problems. Captain James Hay was out with the very serious and (in 1908) life-threatening illness called appendicitis between December and March and round about the same time Jimmy Quinn was out with a septic toe. In addition, Willie Orr the left-back now retired and was replaced by an equally talented left-back from Ayrshire called Jamie Weir, a fast-moving player with a tremendous talent off the field for doing 'Tam O'Shanter' recitations.

Manager Maley beside Young, Somers, McMenemy, Adams, Mitchell, Weir in the middle row. Front row is Hamilton, McLeod, Loney, Hay, Quinn, McNair. In front is the Glasgow Charity Cup, the Scottish Cup and the Glasgow Cup.

Another Ayrshire man, the talismanic Bobby Templeton, fell from favour and left the club, and for the left-wing position, Maley turned once again to Davie Hamilton whose dainty footwork and dribbling skills earned him the nickname of "the dancer".

In a team which had no weaknesses whatsoever, one man stood out. This was James "Napoleon" McMenemy. He earned the name of the little Corsican French general and emperor of 100 years ago because he was a superb tactician. Willie Maley would say that to McMenemy, the football field was a chess board, and his great asset was his ability to see several moves ahead of anyone else. In addition to his reading of the game, Napoleon could also pass with supreme accuracy, he could take on opponents, he could run through a defence and score a goal, he could head a ball, and for a small man, he was able to look after himself on the sometimes rough and tough football field. Yet he remained a modest man and a superb ambassador for the club at this time and in later years as well.

And there were loads of more than adequate reserves around – Willie Kivlichan (who had joined the club from Rangers!), Davie McLean, Johnny Mitchell, Billy Semple to name but four who could have walked into any team and held down a place. But this was a mighty Celtic side. Davie McLean, in particular, who eventually scored more goals than McGrory (and that is saying something!) could not command a regular place.

The season opened with five wins, then followed a sticky spell when Sunny Jim Young was out, and this included a defeat at Pittodrie on the Aberdeen Monday Holiday or "Fast" as it was called locally. But the team bounced back, won the Glasgow Cup Final at the third attempt against Rangers in October, and the only defeat between then and the New Year was at Tynecastle in late November. Celtic were without Davie Hamilton that day, and made the decision to play Quinn on the left wing. This had been Quinn's original position but he was far better in the centre. December saw three fine victories and a disappointing goalless draw at Airdrie which frankly should have been won. Celtic finished the calendar year of 1907 third in the Scottish League behind Dundee and leaders Falkirk, but both they and Rangers had games in hand because of the length of time taken to complete the Glasgow Cup.

It was New Year 1908 that saw Celtic step up a gear with two home wins against Rangers and Aberdeen. Davie

Jimmy "Napoleon" McMenemy

Hamilton and Jimmy McMenemy scored the goals against Rangers in the narrow but convincing 2–1 win at Parkhead on New Year's Day, and then the following day at the same venue, Billy Semple, Jimmy Quinn and Peter Somers scored the goals which beat the "wasps" of Aberdeen. These games were played in fine weather, but the weather then broke down before the game due to be played on 4 January against Queen's Park at Hampden.

After that, however, Celtic really got going again winning games in the League and the Cup, and an aura of invincibility began to develop about them. The absence of Quinn and Hay was hardly noticed and Maley continued his policy of taking them away for training at nice Highland hotels – in this case Tarbet, on Loch Lomond – getting the club to provide good clothes for them to wear, insisting that they entertained the other guests after dinner with songs and recitations, and making them feel good about themselves. Jamie Weir did the recitation, Peter Somers played the piano and everyone else was encouraged to sing Scottish, Irish or Victorian parlour songs like 'Who is Sylvia?'. In the absence of James Hay, "Jamie" or Sunny Jim Young "of the blonde locks and the lanky legs" as the *Dundee Courier* describes him, was the captain and he led by example with his stentorian and famous "Face the ball, Celts!" becoming well known throughout Scotland.

The next defeat (indeed the only defeat between now and the end of the season) came at Dens Park on 28 March. Frankly, Celtic "took a kicking" in this game. Dundee went ahead with a first minute penalty, then Jamie Weir was taken off injured, then Peter Somers missed the whole of the second half through injury. The treatment of Quinn in particular was brutal, and it was hardly surprising that Celtic lost 0–2. Fortunately Celtic did not retaliate, but left the field with a grim determination that such things were never to happen again. In fact, they were still in the best position to win the League for they had games in hand over Falkirk and Dundee.

Wins over Morton and Queen's Park followed, 2–0 in each case, the win over Morton being all the more praiseworthy for McNair and Quinn were playing for Scotland that day, and then on the Holiday Monday, 20 April, after the Scottish Cup win over St Mirren, in excellent weather Celtic took another step towards the League flag with a 6–0 win over Hearts. Jimmy Quinn scored a hat-trick, and the other goals were notched by Jimmy McMenemy, Willie Loney and Davie Hamilton. The Scottish Cup was on show at half-time, and it was now surely only a matter of time before the Scottish League joined it at Celtic Park.

The chance came as soon as Saturday with the trip to Ibrox. This was Rangers' last League game, whereas Celtic, who were a point ahead and had three games left, only had to win this game to make the League Championship mathematically safe. Rangers had bought a famous player, one James Sharp from Woolwich Arsenal, to play against Alec Bennett. Frankly, Bennett the "artful dodger" never allowed Sharp a kick of the ball, and it was Bennett who scored the only goal of the game, won far more comprehensively by Celtic than the 1–0 score would suggest. Once again Quinn was brutally injured by a coarse Rangers defender, but he never retaliated. His reward came at the full-time whistle when Celtic had won their eighth Scottish League flag. It was the second year in a row that they had won the Scottish double.

There were two postscripts to this remarkable season. One was that this year Celtic did not slip up in the Glasgow Charity Cup, but won it handsomely to complete the clean sweep of all the trophies they entered (as happened in 1967). The second frankly defies rational analysis. Alec Bennett suddenly announced that he was leaving to join Rangers. He was a Rangers supporter by nature, a non-Catholic (but that didn't matter, for neither were Young, Hay, McNair, McLean and several others) and perhaps the Ibrox men offered him more money, but why on earth would a man who was the "pet" of the Parkhead crowd and generally recognised as one of the stars of the "greatest show on earth" want to leave Parkhead at this juncture? "There are things that a fella just can't understand" says Sam Weller in *The Pickwick Papers*. This would appear to be one of them.

Scottish Cup Final		
Celtic 5 St Mirren 1	Hampden	18 April
English Cup Final		
Wolves 3 Newcastle United 1	Crystal Palace	25 April
English League		
Manchester United		

CHAPTER 9

"WE WON IT IN A FORTNIGHT"

1908/09

The year 1909 is immediately associated in the minds of students of the history of Scottish football with the infamous Hampden riot at the replay of the Scottish Cup Final between Celtic and Rangers on 17 April. It is important to stress that there was no sectarian element in all this, at least not at the start. There may have been an element of "us v. them" once things got going, but the riot was triggered by the perception that the decision not to play extra-time was because both clubs and the SFA wanted yet another big gate in a potential third game.

It had been an issue that had simmered for some time. The last two Glasgow Cup Finals had taken three games – two tame draws and then the game decided at the third attempt once the crowds began to lessen, and both this year's Glasgow Cup semi-final between Celtic and Rangers, and the Scottish Cup semi-final between Celtic and Clyde had taken two games. Any allegations of collusion or corruption are of course difficult to prove or corroborate – and "fixing" a game would have needed to involve an awful lot of people – but it was a perception that would not go away. Even long after the dreadful events of 1909 had disappeared from public memory, the drawn Scottish Cup Finals between Celtic and Rangers of 1963, 1966 and 1971 still raised a few eyebrows in some quarters.

Irrespective of all this, disorder of that nature could not be tolerated, and the SFA decided to withhold the Scottish Cup in 1909. Hampden Park was of course badly damaged, and they had little option. But how did all this affect the Scottish League? There were those who wanted the Scottish League abandoned that season as well, but fortunately, that extreme option was not pursued. There were still, however, major problems in the fulfilling of the fixtures.

Celtic's League form this year had been patchy. Frankly, with all due respect to his replacements Dan Munro and Willie Kivlichan, Alec Bennett was badly missed. His absence also seems to have a detrimental effect of the play of his good friend Jimmy McMenemy, in the same way as, 10 years ago, Sandy McMahon suffered when Johnny Campbell was not there. Early on in the season, there had been defeats at Dundee and a shocker to St Mirren at home, and then on Boxing Day there had been a rare defeat to Clyde at home as well. The Glasgow Cup Final against Third Lanark had raised two questions. One was the business of why it took the three games, and the other was why in the third game, a team of all that talent suddenly collapsed 0–4 to Neddy Tarbet's competent, but little more than that, side from Cathkin.

Goalkeeper Davie Adams. It would be a year or two before goalkeepers had to wear a different coloured jersey, but Davie's collar is here green to mark him out from the other players.

The Scottish League table at the turn of the year is confusing. Celtic are fourth but they have simply not played enough games – 15 as distinct from the 19 of Rangers and the 21 of Dundee. But Celtic beat Rangers 3–1 at Ibrox on New Year's Day with goals from Davie Hamilton, Jimmy McMenemy and Dan Munro, and then in unfortunate circumstances, lost to Kilmarnock at Rugby Park on 2 January. Goalkeeper Davie Adams had been injured at Ibrox, and as there was no deputy goalkeeper available at short notice, Sunny Jim Young, himself recovering from an injury, took over in goal. He did well there, but was badly missed in his normal position of right-half. A draw followed at Tynecastle, but after that, form began to settle down in the month of February.

March was not so good with a draw at Brockville and a defeat (caused by injuries to Hay and Quinn) to Rangers at Celtic Park on 13 March. This reverse might well have signalled the end of Celtic's title ambitions, had it not been for the fact that they still had so many games left to play, and also that no one strong challenger had emerged with the other teams tending to beat each other. Dundee, in fact, were the best of the rest and had recently hit a good run of form. They were now 10 points ahead of Celtic, but had only four games left to play whereas Celtic had eleven!

Nervous 1–0 wins over Partick Thistle and St Mirren followed, and then in the midweek between the Scottish Cup Final and its replay, Celtic dropped another point to Third Lanark at Cathkin. On the Monday after the Hampden riot, 19 April, a glance at the League table saw Dundee with one game to play on 48 points and Celtic with eight games to play on 39. There were several teams in between them including Rangers, but the title would be between Dundee and Celtic. In 1909, remember there were only two points for a win, a position that would stay unaltered until the 1990s.

It was a ridiculous situation brought about by too many replayed Cup ties. The season had to finish at the end of April, otherwise there would be major problems with players' contracts, etc. and the Scottish League were reluctant to grant an extension. Thus Celtic had to play on 19, 21, 22, 24, 26, 28, 29 and 30 April! It was as well that the SFA had decided to withhold the Scottish Cup and not to have another replay! As it was, eight games in 12 days was not going to be easy. Assuming that Dundee won their last game (against Queen's Park on Saturday, 24 April) Celtic would need 12 points out of a possible 16.

Normally this Celtic team would be expected to do just that. But in such a short time? With injuries and exhaustion? Loney was out, but fortunately Maley had discovered another winner in Joe Dodds. There was a great defence in Adams, McNair and Weir, Sunny Jim was going strong, as indeed was James Hay, while up front the presence of McMenemy, Somers, Hamilton and Quinn meant that anything was possible, in this case backed up by the prolific Dave McLean, a man on whom destiny called in these two weeks.

It all started with a win at Tynecastle, then a 1–1 draw against Hamilton Accies at Parkhead, followed by a 5–1 win over Morton. In that game, Celtic had fielded a young medical student called John Atkinson. He had been loaned from Hamilton Accies the day before (because he was an amateur, this was allowed) and he scored twice! On Saturday, 24 April, while Dundee beat Queen's Park at Ibrox (Hampden was, of course, out of action after the riot) Celtic had bad luck in only getting a draw against Airdrie. Dundee were now finished on 50 points, while Celtic needed six points from four games.

Quinn and McLean were on song as Motherwell were defeated at Parkhead on Monday and Queen's Park at Cathkin on Wednesday. Another two points would do it, but then understandable exhaustion crept in at Easter Road on the Thursday on a heavy pitch and Hibs won 1–0. It all therefore depended on the last game. What would have happened if it had been a draw and both teams equal, no one really seemed to know. A play-off as in 1905? Declared equal champions as in 1891? Goal average? Celtic would have won, but that method was not yet in vogue.

In the event, 6,000 people crowded into the trim little enclosure that was Douglas Park, Hamilton in those days to see Celtic win 2–1 on a fine spring evening. There are reports of the game being watched by ladies in their fine dresses and, in some cases, escorted by military men from the nearby barracks. Celtic summoned up everything they had, and Davie Hamilton scored in the first half and Jimmy McMenemy in the second. Although the Accies scored near the end, Celtic held out to secure their fifth League Championship in a row and their ninth overall.

It must go down as one of Celtic's most epic League Championship victories. The last two weeks were truly remarkable as Maley, perhaps irked by the rumours of corruption and match fixing in Cup ties and certainly upset about there being no Scottish Cup that year, determined to prove that his Celtic team were the greatest of them all. In this, he gloriously succeeded.

As a postscript, the victorious Celtic team immediately went on tour of the Highlands! Hardly surprisingly, however, when they came back, they lost the Glasgow Charity Cup. But they had once again confounded everyone. How long could their dominance of the Scottish League continue?

Scottish Cup Final
Cup Withheld after riot at Hampden on 17 April following two draws, 2-2 and 1-1 against Rangers.

English Cup Final
Manchester United 1 Bristol City 0 Crystal Palace 24 April

English League
Newcastle United

CHAPTER 10

END OF AN ERA

1909/10

Season 1909/10 was fated to be the last of Celtic's famous six-in-a-row League winning run. There had been some fantastic football played, but all good things must come to an end, it was said. There was something almost symbolic about that fact that King Edward VII died in 1910 as well, but of far more direct political relevance to the Irish community in Glasgow was the prolonged, ongoing battle between the Liberals and the House of Lords, for the House of Lords had been the main obstacle to Home Rule for Ireland, and still were.

The events at the end of the previous season had their effect on the summer. Letters appeared in newspapers deploring hooliganism at football matches in the wake of the Scottish Cup Final including a few crackpots who wanted the game "stopped altogether", but the Celtic community talked about little other than the way the League was won. There seemed no stopping this Celtic side with great men like Sunny Jim, Napoleon and Jimmy Quinn feted and talked about endlessly – and showing, as yet, no signs of ageing.

Celtic began 1909/10 with a couple of hiccups. There were defeats at Easter Road to Hibs and at Cappielow to Morton, but a significant win (although no one realised it at the time) would be the defeat of Falkirk at Celtic Park on 21 August. Falkirk would emerge to be the main challengers to Celtic this season in the same way as it had been Dundee the previous season. Celtic's season had begun eccentrically on the night of Wednesday, 17 August, Hay, Quinn and McMenemy scoring the goals which beat Hamilton Accies before a surprisingly meagre crowd, not yet attuned to the football season, and then on the Saturday before a much larger crowd McMenemy and Willie Kivlichan scored the goals which defeated the "Bairns".

Round about this time, Maley made a permanent change to the forward line. Peter Somers had been a great, if occasionally underestimated, member of this team but now Peter was over 30 and slowing down. He was called the "powder monkey" after the small young boys who crawled inside cannons on board ship to load them. This was seen as the symbolic supplying of the ammunition for Jimmy Quinn.

Peter had had one or two poor games, and Maley introduced a taller, more muscular miner from Fife called Peter Johnstone. Johnstone, fated to lose his life in the Great War, would prove to be a player of outstanding versatility, winning honours for the club at left-half and centre-half, but it was at inside left that he started, fitting in seamlessly to that great team.

Hampden had been sufficiently repaired to allow the Glasgow Cup Final to be played there in October and Celtic duly beat Rangers 1–0. From then on Celtic

Peter Johnstone.

played consistently good football, with very few thrashings of the opposition but doing enough to win and scoring goals regularly (Jimmy Quinn, of course!) to ensure that New Year was reached with Celtic on top of the League, closely followed by Falkirk, and these two well ahead of everyone else. The Christmas Day game against Kilmarnock at Rugby Park had seen a remarkable individual goal scored by Jimmy Quinn where he had beaten several men on the muddy pitch and scored brilliantly. It was a goal which earned plaudits in the *Glasgow Herald* for "the game was going all against his side" as "he shot on the run with amazing power from 25 yards", "the goalkeeper seeing the ball all the way without having a chance to stay its progress". Christmas Day in Kilmarnock was never quite the same again after that!

New Year's Day at Celtic Park saw a 1–1 draw against Rangers, a tough game involving an injury to McMenemy. The draw allowed Falkirk to catch up with Celtic, and then at the end of January, after three satisfactory results, Celtic went down to St Mirren at Love Street in a nasty match on a hard ground which saw numerous injuries, and Sunny Jim sent off "for allowing his tongue to wag too freely". This meant that if Falkirk won their games in hand, they would be above Celtic.

But bad weather, International commitments and the Scottish Cup now intervened, and by the time that Celtic played their next League match, it was the middle of March. It was the second of a remarkable run of five fixtures against Glasgow teams, none of them being Rangers. Celtic were now out of the Scottish Cup (to Clyde on 12 March) but nine League matches remained. The first such game was a Wednesday afternoon game at Celtic Park against Third Lanark, and an undistinguished 2–0 win with a penalty kick converted by Jimmy Quinn and another scored by Peter Johnstone.

Saturday, 19 March saw Celtic beat Queen's Park at Hampden 1–0. Without Quinn and Hay, who were playing for Scotland in Ireland that day, the depleted Celtic side still won with a goal from the honest journeyman Willie Kivlichan. Falkirk had won that day at Kilmarnock, but as they had drawn against Hibs a couple of weeks earlier, they were now two points behind Celtic with the same amount of games played. 26 March against Partick Thistle was a great 3–1 victory for Celtic, with Jimmy Quinn once again rampant as he scored a hat-trick, but still Celtic could not shake off Falkirk who proved their Championship credentials by beating Scottish Cup finalists Clyde 6–1 that day.

The League race was becoming quite exciting at this time with the young Falkirk side pressing hard, and Celtic beginning to struggle on occasion and relying too much on Jimmy Quinn to score the goals. April 23 was scheduled for Celtic's visit to Brockville (it had been postponed in February) but in the meantime Celtic hit a run of form and just kept winning. Celtic won three home games in early

D. Adams R. Davis *Trainer* J. Quinn W. Loney A. M'Nair T. M'Ateer P. Johnstone J. Young J. M'Menemy J. Dodds
A. M'Atee J. Hastie J. Hay *Captain* J. Mitchell D. Hamilton
CELTIC FOOTBALL CLUB, 1910-11
SCOTTISH CHAMPIONS
1892-3 1893-4 1895-6 1897-8 1904-5 1905-6 1906-7 1907-8 1908-9 1909-10

April against Clyde, Morton and Aberdeen and Quinn scored in them all, a hat-trick against Clyde and one each in the other two. But it was the day of 9 April which swung the League decisively in favour of Celtic.

While the Scottish Cup Final between Dundee and Clyde was ending in a 2–2 draw at Ibrox, Celtic beat Aberdeen 2–0 at Parkhead, and Falkirk could only draw with St Mirren at Brockville, their cause not helped by a missed penalty. Draws were Falkirk's bane that year, for they drew eight times. All this meant that a draw would give Celtic the League title when they went to Falkirk on 23 April, but even if they didn't, they had another two games left. Unfortunately for Celtic and their large travelling support which descended on Falkirk from very early on as the trains pulled in from Glasgow, Falkirk turned on a sparkling performance and won 2–0.

It only delayed the inevitable, however. It was now on to Celtic Park on the Monday. Celtic needed only a point and they duly got it but in the most anticlimactic way imaginable with a dull 0–0 draw against Hibs before a paltry

Scottish Cup Final		
Dundee 2 Clyde 1	Ibrox	20 April
(after 2-2 and 0-0 draws on 9 and 16 April at Ibrox)		
English Cup Final		
Newcastle United 2 Barnsley 0	Goodison	28 April
(after 1-1 draw on 23 April at Crystal Palace)		
English League		
Aston Villa		

2,000 crowd (it was not the Holiday Monday, unfortunately). Quinn had been injured at Falkirk and was out, and his absence was sorely missed, but fortunately reserve goalkeeper Willie Duncan (Davie Adams had been out for weeks with pneumonia) had a good game and defied the Hibs forwards.

The six-in-a-row Championship was thus gained, albeit not in the way that Maley (who also celebrated his 42nd birthday that day, 25 April) would have wanted. But that is not to denigrate the achievement. League Championships are not all about champagne and caviar. They have to be worked hard for, and sometimes the way they are achieved is far from glamorous. Celtic had now won the Scottish League Championship 10 times in the competition's 20-year history. Rangers had won it four times and had shared it once with Dumbarton. Hearts had won it twice, Hibs, Third Lanark and Dumbarton once each.

CHAPTER 11

WAR? WAR? DINNAE BE DAFT!

1913/14

Season 1913/14 was one of the greatest in the history of the club. Celtic had had three "years off", as it were, from winning the League but the intervening years had hardly been failures, for the Scottish Cup had been won in 1911 and 1912 and, although 1913 had been barren apart from the Glasgow Charity Cup, a new team was emerging out of the old. Maley in fact was replacing one world-beating team with another.

Men like Adams, Loney, Hay, Hamilton and Somers had gone. Jimmy Quinn was reluctant to give up, but injuries and the ageing process had caught up. New men had, however, come in their place. Peter Johnstone, for example, had now developed into a mighty centre-half, Joe Dodds was now a superb attacking left-back and the left flank was completed by Johnny McMaster, "of the melancholy countenance" at left-half and Johnny Browning a superb left-winger. On the right wing was a boy from Croy by the name of Andy McAtee, a sturdy youth with legs like "those of a billiard table", and at centre-forward a lad by the name of Jimmy McColl was called upon to take the place of the great Jimmy Quinn after the likeable Ebenezer Owers had proved to be not quite up to it.

This picture showing Sunny Jim holding the Scottish Cup won on Thursday, 14 April was taken two days later, prior to the game which would win the Scottish League. Back row: W. Maley manager, McMaster, Dodds, Shaw, McNair, Johnstone, McColl, W. Quinn trainer. Front row: McAtee, Gallacher, Young, McMenemy, Browning.

"Sunny Jim" Young, Eck "the icicle" McNair, and Jimmy "Napoleon" McMenemy were still there, as productive as ever, but two real legends had appeared. One is cagey about using the word "legend", for it is much over-used in modern football writing, but it is difficult to refrain from using the word about goalkeeper Charlie Shaw and the boy from Donegal, Patsy Gallacher. Shaw had recently joined the club from Queen's Park Rangers in 1913, and by the end of the season would be recognised as a goalkeeper second to none, while 1913/14 was the season which first brought the world's attention to the wiles and trickery of the great Patsy Gallacher.

The Celtic support in summer 1913 were not happy people. The club was celebrating its 25th anniversary, ironically after one of the worst ever seasons. (Curiously, 50 years later, the 75th season in 1963 would be similarly barren.) The sustained success of 1904–1910 had gone and the current team were even being compared unfavourably to men like Sandy McMahon and Dan Doyle. Celtic supporters are traditionally moany, unhappy, impatient and intolerant when things are not going well. By the turn of the year, the grousers had been quietened, and by April even the most pessimistic and lugubrious were singing the praises of this tremendous team.

Although McMenemy and McNair were both out for a spell, the replacements were adequate and Maley was more or less able to count on the same team every week. This was significant because one of the characteristics of this squad was their knowledge and understanding of each other. This is, of course, an indispensable quality in a good team, and Maley worked hard to develop the team spirit for which good Celtic teams are famous. He continued his traditions of "away days" at Seamill Hydro and other such places, with emphasis on hard work at training, backed up with good food, games of snooker and table tennis, and loads of singing and piano playing to entertain and charm the other guests.

The Scottish League First Division now contained 20 clubs, something that many people considered was perhaps too many, and yet it only meant 38 games – the same as in the Premier League in 2018! The season did not start particularly well for Celtic with two successive defeats in mid-September, one to St Mirren at home and then another two days later to Hearts on the Edinburgh Holiday Monday. Then they lost to Third Lanark in the Glasgow Cup in October. But then the team rallied. A 1–0 win at Pittodrie with the goal scored by Sunny Jim, of all people, was the beginning of an unbeaten run which lasted all the way through the winter until 28 February, when they lost at Falkirk on a day when several men were away on International duty. All this was impressive enough, but when one considers that all this time they only conceded one goal – to Jimmy Scott of Raith Rovers on 13 December – one gets an idea of how good the defence of Shaw, McNair and Dodds was.

There were a couple of disappointing 0–0 draws in all this, against Motherwell and Partick Thistle, but there were also some great performances, not least at Celtic Park on New Year's Day when a 4–0 hammering of the city rivals was characterised by a great goal from Napoleon just before half-time when he beat five defenders before hammering home from the edge of the box. The Parkhead crowd, upbeat and deliriously happy, nevertheless lost no opportunity to jeer and mock ex-favourite Alec Bennett, now playing ineffectively for Rangers at inside-left and barely able to get at a kick of the ball, such was the total command of his direct opponent Jimmy Young. But the victory was made possible only through the fine saving of Charlie Shaw in Rangers' early onslaught.

Johnny Browning's only goal of the game at Dens Park on 17 January was a significant day in Celtic's march to the title, as both Rangers and Hearts dropped points that day, and the slip up at Falkirk was soon recovered from. Wednesday, 1 April saw a good 3–1 win at Cathkin with two goals from Patsy Gallacher and one from Jimmy McMenemy, and then the following Wednesday (on the intervening Saturday, McMenemy had engineered a great Scottish victory over England at Hampden) at Kilmarnock a narrow win with the only goal of the game coming from Patsy Gallacher put Celtic on the cusp of the Championship at the same time as they were preparing for the Scottish Cup Final against Hibs.

It was called the "Irish" Cup Final in some newspapers, but it ended 0–0. It was a disappointing encounter which raised once again the rumours of a "fix" for a big gate in the replay, but the Easter Monday fixtures saw Celtic beat Queen's Park 5–0 in the League, while Rangers could only draw at Partick Thistle. Celtic won the Scottish Cup Final replay 4–0 on the Thursday, and then on the Saturday before an exultant Celtic crowd at Parkhead faced Hibs again, this time to win the Scottish League.

It would be wrong to minimise the effect of politics on the Celtic support at this time. Lloyd George had drawn the teeth of the House of Lords in the struggle for Irish Home Rule, but a far more serious obstacle lay in the Orangemen of the North who, bigoted and stubborn as always, were determined to resist. Civil war looked a distinct possibility, but for the Celtic supporters in Scotland in 1914 there was little other than triumph to celebrate.

The Double was thus clinched (emulating 1907 and 1908) with a rather easy 3–0 win over a dispirited Hibs. McMenemy scored twice and McColl once after the Scottish Cup has been displayed at the start. It was an excellent season for Celtic, and well were they worthy of the paeans of praise in the newspapers and in the conversation of their fans. The team then went on to win the Glasgow Charity Cup as well (only their failure in the Glasgow Cup in October preventing a 1908-style clean sweep) and then in early summer Celtic went on a very successful tour of Germany and the Austro-Hungarian Empire, the only problems coming from Burnley, the winners of the English Cup. Great friendships were made with the locals, and although there was always some degree of tension in the air about the Irish problem in Great Britain, no one ever in his wildest nightmares imagined that there would ever be any kind of war in Europe in 1914. Boat trips down the *Rhein*, lovely *fräuleins*, good food, charming hosts all in awe of the great Celtic. What could be the problem?

Scottish Cup Final		
Celtic 4 Hibs 0	Ibrox	16 April
(after 0-0 draw at Ibrox on 11 April)		
English Cup Final		
Burnley 1 Liverpool 0	Crystal Palace	25 April
English League		
Blackburn Rovers		

CHAPTER 12

UNDER THE FLAG OF WAR

1914/15

By the time that the first game of the 1914/15 League season was played – a 0–2 defeat to Hearts at Tynecastle – the country had been at war for a week and a half. Contrary to the beliefs perpetrated by some historians, who said that war was inevitable and had been brewing for months if not years, 4 August caught everyone by surprise and was brought about by incompetent diplomacy, highlighting the folly of Great Britain having an alliance with the Czar of Russia, for example! And then of course, the Germans invaded Belgium!

The effect on Scottish football, however, was fairly drastic. International matches and the Scottish Cup were immediately shelved, footballers had to have a job in a "war-related industry" before they were allowed to play football, football could only be played on a Saturday or a holiday, and football matches were the target of army recruitment, who tried to persuade the gullible to join up "before it was too late".

Celtic's 0–2 defeat on opening day to Hearts was an unfortunate one, in that it allowed the myth to develop that Hearts would have won the Championship in 1915 if their players had not decided more or less en masse to enlist in November. While no one wishes to take anything away from the brave, if perhaps misguided, Hearts players who joined up, the facts do not support the case that Hearts were seriously depleted in the 1915 season. Their players were virtually all available for their games in that season, for they were still in Scotland doing their basic training. Arguably, they would have been fitter than normal with loads of exercise, fresh air and good army food!

Still less was there any justification for the sneer that Celtic were "war dodgers". Peter Johnstone, Celtic's centre-half, was fated to die at Arras in 1917, several other lesser-known Celtic players would meet a similar fate, and there was no monopoly of suffering in the so-called "Footballers Battalion" which, in any case, contained men from teams like Falkirk and Raith Rovers as well as Hearts.

That said, credit must be given to Mr Maley, himself the son of a soldier, for ensuring that most of his great team of 1914 found themselves jobs in "war related" industries, usually within travelling distance of Celtic Park so that they would be available for a Saturday afternoon. Maley was also punctilious about sending a telegram to the War Office with Celtic's result so that soldiers could know about the fortune of their team within an hour of the full-time whistle if the War Office passed on the news timeously. Thus it came about that among Scottish soldiers Patsy Gallacher was "the most talked about man in the trenches".

Celtic in 1914/15
Back Row: Andy McAtee, Charlie Shaw, Johnny McMaster. Middle Row: Joe Cassidy, Alec McNair, Johnny Browning, Jimmy McMenemy, Patsy Gallacher, Trainer Willie Quinn. Front Row: Willie Maley, Peter Johnstone, Tom White, Jimmy Young, James Kelly, Joe Dodds, Michael Dunbar

While hysterical letters poured in to the *Glasgow Herald* and *The Scotsman* demanding the suspension of football, the season continued. As often happened with Celtic, there were a few early reverses. Points were dropped at St Mirren, Hibs and Raith Rovers, and there was a particular shocker at Somerset Park where the team went down 0–1, while there was also a disturbing reverse to Clyde in the Glasgow Cup, the result that was said to "have caused consternation in the ranks" of the British Expeditionary Force.

But once Celtic adapted to the demands of wartime football, which meant that it was very difficult to organise any kind of training session, for example, form began to pick up. The veteran Jimmy Quinn (now in his late 30s) tried to make a comeback, playing the occasional game but his replacement Jimmy McColl, soon to be called "the Sniper" became very impressive in the forward line. With men like Gallacher and McMenemy on either side of him, it was difficult not to score goals! The next reverse after the hesitant early start would be on New Year's Day at Ibrox where, in foul weather of wind and rain, a crowd of 30,000 (many home on leave and wearing the khaki) saw a 2–1 win for Rangers. This reverse now meant that Celtic were in trouble because Hearts were six points ahead and had a game in hand into the bargain.

But the reverse at Ibrox was the last defeat of the season. Celtic now won four games in January over Clyde, Kilmarnock, Partick Thistle and Falkirk before Hearts came to Celtic Park on 30 January. Hearts had in the meantime drawn twice to Falkirk and Third Lanark. A crowd of 45,000 (which says a great deal about how popular football was in wartime) saw the game at Celtic Park. It turned out to be Jimmy Quinn's last game but even his presence could not bring the victory that Celtic craved. Graham scored for Hearts early on, and Andy McAtee equalised in the second half, but Hearts defence held out. They were "fortunate in effecting a draw" according to the *Glasgow Herald* but they were now four points ahead of Celtic and both teams had played 27 games out of the 38.

It was a situation analogous to 1968 where all that Celtic could do was to keep winning their own games, and hope that their opponents would crack. It was better, for psychological reasons, for Celtic to win all their games comfortably. This they proceeded to do. 5–1 over Hibs, 4–0 over Third Lanark and a couple of 3–0s brought much needed comfort for the Celtic fans and piled the pressure on Hearts. As it turned out, it was Rangers who produced the first crack in the Tynecastle edifice. Rangers had had a poor season so far, but on 20 February, they travelled to Edinburgh and with 10 minutes to go were winning 4–0. Hearts staged a late rally but could only register three goals. Meanwhile, across in Glasgow, Celtic with a good goal from Jimmy McColl, beat a determined Dumbarton side 1–0.

Only two points in it now, and if there had been a crack in the Tynecastle edifice, the water began to seep in the following week when they went to Easter Road and came back with only a draw. They had twice been behind, and twice Hibs equalised. Celtic were at Firhill that day before an astonishing crowd of 30,000 and won 2–0 with a goal from McColl and a penalty sunk by Joe Dodds. "McMenemy was outstanding" according to *The Scotsman*.

There was now a "spring in the step" of the Celts and next week 6 March, they beat Hibs 5–1, although they were disappointed to hear that Hearts had now apparently recovered from their poor results and beaten Dumbarton 4–1. By a quirk of the fixtures, Celtic were without a game on 13 March, but Hearts dropped another point, this time to Airdrie. The following week, Celtic missed another game, Celtic Park being used for a League International which had surprisingly been allowed, but Hearts beat Partick Thistle 3–1. On 27 March both teams won, and thus we entered April with Celtic having five games to play, Hearts three, and Hearts now four points ahead. It was certainly an exciting race. If Celtic won their games in hand, it would be level pegging,

But April and the better weather won it for Celtic. Celtic won four of their five games (the last one at Motherwell was a draw in a game that no longer mattered) scoring 11 goals without reply, whereas Hearts simply blew up. A feckless 0–0 draw at Pittodrie on 3 April while Celtic beat Airdrie 3–0 and then Queen's Park by the same score on the Holiday Monday, meant that Celtic's narrow 1–0 win over Aberdeen (the goal scored by the apparently omnipotent McMenemy) on 10 April and Hearts' woeful 0–2 defeat at Morton were enough to give Celtic the lead. To win the Scottish League flag for the twelfth time, Celtic then went to Cathkin on 17 April and treated a large crowd of 20,000 to a display of Celtic attacking football

There was no Scottish Cup played that year, but the English tournaments were won as follows:

English Cup Final

Sheffield United 3 Chelsea 0	Old Trafford	24 April

English League

Everton

at its best with two goals from Johnny Browning and one each from McMenemy and McColl. It showed why Celtic deserved to be champions and took everyone's mind off what was going on in the Dardanelles.

Celtic completed their season by winning the Glasgow Charity Cup beating Rangers 3–2 in the Final on 8 May, the day after German torpedoes had sunk the *Lusitania* off the coast of Ireland. The war was now a very serious matter indeed.

CHAPTER 13

TWO IN A DAY

1915/16

The war intensified in 1915/16 and so did Celtic's domination of Scottish football. A new dynamic which entered the equation in early 1916 was the introduction of conscription, something that was not perhaps resisted as fiercely, or as universally, as one would have expected. There were exemptions and deferments, of course, and tribunals were set up to decide who had to go and who didn't. Football players, of course, like everyone else, were likely to be called up, and so too were the fans.

Two areas where conscription impacted on the Celtic community were on Glasgow's Clyde where labour unrest was common, and of course, Ireland. The government had, wisely, not yet introduced conscription in Ireland, but the clear impression that it was being contemplated was definitely a catalyst for the events of Easter 1916.

Over the summer of 1915 there had been a distinct diminution of Scottish football. The Second Division of the Scottish League had folded, with most of the smaller teams unable to field a credible team or having serious problems with the logistics of wartime transport. In England, the English League and the English Cup had been suspended and replaced with local competitions to cut down on the travelling, but the Scottish League, to its credit, refused to give in to emotional blackmail and continued in spite of the obvious problems.

The argument put forward by Maley and others was that football was an entertainment, and that soldiers home on leave and the workers in the munitions industries (which were sometimes no less dangerous than the life of a soldier or a sailor) deserved something to cheer them up for morale reasons. The infant cinema was enjoying a boost in wartime circumstances as well, as indeed were the Music Hall and the theatre. If Celtic's main plank for their existence in wartime was to boost morale, in this they certainly succeeded, for Patsy Gallacher and Jimmy McMenemy were enough to assuage any broken heart or worried brow!

Celtic began the 1915/16 season with 10 straight wins. They included the Glasgow Cup won at Hampden Park before 70,000 and there were several remarkable features of this game. One was that although the score was only 2–1, Rangers supporters left early en masse, so dominant were the Patsy Gallacher inspired Celts, and another was that Joe Dodds and Jimmy McMenemy both played that day, even though each of them had had a brother recently killed in the ongoing Battle of Loos.

League form had been consistently good. Airdrie and Clyde were both beaten 5–0, Hibs 4–0 and possibly the best game of the early part of the season was the one played at Dens Park, Dundee on 18 September, where the home side put

Patsy Gallacher, the greatest of them all.

up a plucky fight, but goals by Johnny Browning and Patsy Gallacher saw Celtic through. The crowd was close to 20,000, and they were mightily impressed.

But as often happens with even the best of teams, a bad patch was hit. In late October to early November, three games out of four were lost. One was a shocker to St Mirren at home – irrational and inexplicable, the other two were slightly more predictable reverses at Tynecastle and Ibrox, Rangers thereby getting some sort of revenge for their Glasgow Cup defeat. The St Mirren game was lost by two defensive errors – Eck McNair making one of his rare mistakes and passing the ball across the field to Joe Dodds and having the ball intercepted, and the other goal came in the last minute when Charlie Shaw came out of his goal in a desperate attempt to launch the ball for an equaliser but was dispossessed.

The 0–3 reverse at Ibrox was not as one-sided as it sounded – Patsy Gallacher hit the post with a penalty kick, for example, and the defeat at Hearts, also narrow and even unfair, was the last defeat that Celtic would see for some time – 21 April 1917, in fact, 63 games in the future, would be the next time they lost. Sunny Jim was missing for this game at Tynecastle and his absence was a significant one. All this meant that Celtic now had the same points as Rangers, but had played two more games.

A sign of a good side however, whether in peace or in war, is how quickly they can recover from a bad spell. This side had very few problems. By the end of 1915, they had lost only another two goals (and that was in a 6–2 thrashing of Queen's Park) as they beat Kilmarnock, Raith Rovers, Queen's Park, Ayr United and Partick Thistle before the hammering of Airdrie 6–0 at Celtic Park on Christmas Day. There may have been a game or two of football against the Germans in some parts of the Front that day, but most Scottish soldiers were talking about Patsy Gallacher's hat-trick. The *Daily Record* says that Celtic went through the Airdrie defence like "water through a riddle" and singles out the magnificent half-back play of Young, Johnstone and McMaster and, in a strange and somewhat illogical phrase "no wonder the forwards had a picnic, they gave a perfect waltzing lesson".

All this meant that Celtic were now top of the League, although Rangers with games in hand could equal them. The New Year's Day clash saw 60,000 at Celtic Park and the consensus of opinion was that, on the heavy pitch, Celtic were by far the better team with good goals from McAtee and McColl and Rangers indebted to an own goal spinning viciously off Eck McNair's foot for a draw. It meant however that Celtic and Rangers entered 1916 neck and neck.

But Rangers now imploded, as they often do when they realise that Celtic have a better side. As early as 3 January, the Holiday Monday, while Celtic, even without the injured McMenemy, beat Clyde comfortably 3–1 at Shawfield, Rangers lost 0–1 to Partick Thistle and by the end of January, Rangers had lost at Dundee and drawn at Motherwell while Celtic were sweeping all before them with Patsy Gallacher "supplying the ammunition to the Sniper" (Jimmy McColl) in the military imagery of the day. McColl scored four against Hamilton, and right-winger Andy McAtee, another boy from Croy, the home of Jimmy Quinn, was also in great form scoring a hat-trick against Dumbarton.

> The Kaiser, they say, only once saw him play
> And remarked, it is said "Dearie me.
> My German artillery's only fit for the pillory
> They can't shoot like young McAtee!"

It was scintillating stuff, but the manner in which the Scottish League was won that year was totally remarkable. Bad weather on 25 March saw the inevitable postponement of the game at Motherwell, something that raised an immediate problem over when the game could be played. DORA (the Defence of the Realm Act) seemed to preclude midweek games, the season had to finish by 30 April and the Holiday Monday of 24 April was already taken up with the game against Third Lanark. Sunday football, even in the exceptional circumstances of the war, could not be countenanced – although Celtic, less obsessed with Calvinism than most, apparently suggested it – and the only thing that could be done was to play two games on the one day! Thus Celtic would play Raith Rovers in the afternoon of Saturday, 15 April and then travel by charabanc to Motherwell for an early evening kick-off. Both teams would be exhausted (Motherwell were due to play Ayr United that afternoon as well), but if Celtic got their four points, they would be League Champions.

This was no problem to the Celtic side who first beat a severely depleted Raith Rovers 6–0, (a hat-trick for Patsy Gallacher!) then won 3–1 at Motherwell with goals from McMenemy, Browning and a penalty from Joe Dodds. There was only one change with Joe Cassidy replacing Joe O'Kane. The other 10 played both games with a relish emanating from the inspirational captaincy of Sunny Jim who, according to legend, spent the Saturday evening looking for a third team to play!

The *Daily Record* is extremely impressed. The game finished in "the pale moonlight" for the "magnetic presence of the Celtic put life and mettle into the heels of Motherwell" (who had lost to Ayr in the afternoon) and a great game ensued, but Celtic were the better side throughout, and duly earned the plaudits even of the august *Glasgow Herald*.

The rest of 1916 was not great for Great Britain with the Dublin Rising the week after Celtic's great feat, then the Battle of Jutland and the Battle of the Somme, both of them, no matter how they were disguised, unmitigated disasters involving much unnecessary loss of life. Football almost seems irrelevant in such a context, but it was such a vital component in the life of those who lived through such desperate days.

The Scottish Cup, English Cup and English League were all in abeyance

CHAPTER 14

A LONG, LONG TRAIL AWINDING

1916/17

That there was no major disturbance against the war in Glasgow and Scotland in summer 1916 must be put down to the success of British propaganda. Newspapers, somehow or other, seemed to be able to convince everyone that the British were winning the Somme offensive – in fact, it was a colossal defeat with a totally unacceptable amount of casualties – and the Irish question was deliberately portrayed in a confused sort of way with emotive words like "rebels" and "criminals" used to describe those now known as "patriots" and even "heroes". Such protests about the war that there were – the Rent Strike and the ongoing industrial trouble on the Clyde, for example – were often eschewed or minimised in the press. And the great John McLean was demonised.

What could not be hidden, however, was the continuing supremacy of Celtic Football Club who did not lose a game until 21 April 1917, some 63 games since they had lost their last one! What made their success this year all the more remarkable was that they did it without several men who had performed so well in 1916. Peter Johnstone and Johnny McMaster had enlisted, Sunny Jim Young suffered an injury which effectively finished his long and incredibly successful career, and then in the middle of the season, Celtic were without Patsy Gallacher, banned by the Scottish League for being fined for "bad timekeeping" in his job in the shipyards, and nothing to do with football! (This was seen by Celtic supporters as an attempt to stop Celtic winning four League Championships in a row. It failed lamentably!)

Jimmy "Sniper" McColl.

The loss of a whole half-back line (and what a half-back line Young, Johnstone and McMaster had been!) meant that a new one of Wilson, McStay and Brown emerged. Willie McStay would, of course, in time become a Parkhead legend, but Jimmy Wilson and Hugh Brown are lesser-known characters in Celtic history. 1917 was their moment, however.

The game in which Sunny Jim was injured was on 30 September. It was Celtic's seventh win in a row, and was a 1–0 win over Hearts at Celtic Park. The report of the game in the *Daily Record* has no account of Sunny being carried off, but it was certainly his last ever game. It appears that he had injured his knee in the first game of the season (a 5–1 victory against St Mirren at Paisley) but instead of resting it, he was determined to keep playing, and the team having beaten Rangers in the semi-final of the Glasgow Cup, he was very keen on another Glasgow Cup medal. But he must have aggravated it against Hearts, and the pain got too bad even for a man like Sunny. An operation in February failed to solve the problem, and Sunny, now obliged to walk with a limp and sometimes a walking stick, was finished with football.

Even without Young, Celtic kept on winning. They duly lifted the Glasgow Cup in October 1916, using the services of Peter Johnstone who was home on leave, and although there were three draws in October, and one in November, they reached the New Year still unbeaten and with many fine performances to their credit, conceding very few goals (only one in five games in December) and scoring plenty with Sniper McColl and Johnny Browning finding the net frequently.

It is a shame that Browning's best years coincided with the Great War, for he was a fine player and much underrated by historians. A wild character off the field and after the war involved in a match-fixing scandal (not with Celtic), he was nevertheless a great asset to Celtic during the war years.

The war continued. The Somme offensive was eventually given up in November with no one any further forward. The Germans half-heartedly put out peace proposals but they were rejected, and December 1916 saw a major change at the top with Lloyd George, that charismatic, occasionally unpopular but never insignificant Welshman, now Prime Minister and promising more radical action. Food shortages were now apparent – Britain never really came anywhere near to starvation, but some foods were unobtainable – and such were the problems of transport that Raith Rovers, Dundee and Aberdeen were asked to withdraw from the Scottish League at the end of the season.

After the New Year, Celtic were prone to draws. This was the time when Patsy Gallacher was suffering his draconian suspension for bad timekeeping, and it was noticeable that once he returned in February, results picked up. The New Year's Day game at Ibrox was a 0–0 draw. It was a day of heavy rain and the 50,000 crowd including soldiers on leave saw a miserable game with "Waverley" of the *Daily Record* in no doubt that the presence of Patsy Gallacher would have made all the difference. As it was, "Napoleon was very tricky" but the best player seems to have been "the Stenhousemuir icicle" Eck McNair.

There were another three depressing draws in January, but Celtic still ended the month on top of the table, although there were surprise challengers in Morton, a club who had benefitted from the presence of star English players based nearby on the Clyde. This included Stanley Seymour, a man who, after the war, was destined to become a real legend with Newcastle United. Celtic went there on 10 February for a game that would be as close as any in determining the League champions.

The *Daily Record* is ecstatic about this game. It was like the old times with a "packed enclosure", loads of tackles (some of them rather brutal) and excitement to the end. Celtic scored the only goal of the game when young Adam McLean, playing only his second game for the club, made space and found Sniper McColl to score. Celtic's heroes were in the defence, notably Charlie Shaw who saved a penalty from Stanley Seymour and then was injured as Seymour followed up. Patsy Gallacher was brutally brought down by Morton's Jackie Wright, but then Wright was quoted in the *Daily Record* as saying, "Isn't Gallacher a great wee player? The harder you hit him, the quicker he is up!", which one supposes is a great compliment for the diminutive Irishman, who also at one point had to be separated by the referee when he and Seymour had an altercation.

From then on, Celtic experienced few problems that season. There was a thriller of a 2–2 draw at Rugby Park (Celtic needing a last minute equaliser from Jimmy McMenemy to preserve their record), a goalless draw at Pittodrie (McMenemy and Gallacher were unavailable to travel for work reasons) but apart from that, Celtic won all their games. McColl scored 4 in a 6–1 demolition of Hamilton on 10 March, and 31,000 saw Celtic beat St Mirren 3–0 at Celtic Park on 31 March.

7 April was the day that it all happened for Celtic. It was a significant time in the history of the war as well, for the USA had the day before announced their intervention in the war in response to Germany's unrestricted submarine warfare in the Atlantic. This was obviously good news, and Celtic travelled to Dumbarton knowing that a win for Celtic and a defeat for Rangers would guarantee the League for Celtic for the fourth successive year.

They lost an early goal but "brainy McMenemy marshalled his forwards skilfully" and Celtic fought back with an equalising goal from Browning, before a "wriggling run" from Gallacher set up McColl for what was a virtual tap-in. Joe Dodds then converted a penalty to give Celtic a 3–1 victory. Then the really good news came a couple of minutes after the final whistle with a telegram to the effect that Third Lanark had won 2–0 at Ibrox, and that Celtic could not be caught. They had won their fourteenth Scottish League title.

Thus the defeat to Kilmarnock on 21 April did not really matter and Celtic completed another clean sweep of the Scottish honours when Jimmy McColl scored the only goal of the game to beat Queen's Park in the Final of the Glasgow Charity Cup. Even in the extenuating circumstances of the First Word War and all its horrors, this was a fine performance by the team, and the supporters were once again delighted.

But in the early days of June came the news that Maley and Celtic had all dreaded. The death of Peter Johnstone at Arras was confirmed. Peter was one of the many soldiers with "no known grave", a euphemism for the fact that he had been blown to smithereens. It was that kind of a war, and there was no end in prospect. But at least for Celtic supporters in the middle of all this madness, there was something to be happy about.

No other national trophies were competed for in 1917

CHAPTER 15

APRES LA GUERRE FINI

1918/19

Celtic missed out on the title of 1918. Round about the time of the Ludendorff spring offensive when the Germans almost won the war, Celtic failed to do better than draw with Motherwell at Celtic Park, and lost out to Rangers. Summer 1918 was as bloody as any, but eventually the overwhelming strength of the Allies won through, the Ludendorff offensive was stalled, the Americans arrived in strength and the tide was turned. But when the football season began again in August, the war still had a few awful months to run.

Team selection was now even more chaotic with even fewer young men around, now that the "comb-out" had begun and more and more reluctant conscriptees were forced to go to France, the Aegean and Mesopotamia. Celtic lost Andy McAtee, Joe Dodds and Willie McStay, for example, to the forces. But Celtic still had Patsy Gallacher, and as long as he was around, there was always a chance that something could happen.

But McMenemy was not there, having apparently been moved to Belfast for some essential war work. We now enter a dark phase of Napoleon's life, for just about the time that the war ended, Jimmy like so many others fell ill with the Spanish influenza, the phenomenon which killed, worldwide, more than the war itself. Jimmy's dose was particularly virulent and round about the time that the Armistice was signed on 11 November, his illness reached a crisis. Fortunately for Celtic and humanity, Napoleon survived.

The start of the season had been satisfactory for Celtic, although no more than that. They lost twice in October, both times to Rangers, once in the Glasgow Cup Final and once in the Scottish League 0–3 to Rangers at Celtic Park. The attendance on 19 October was down to 36,000, a good 20,000 short of what might have been expected a year or so ago, and they saw a very makeshift Celtic side without even goalkeeper Charlie Shaw in the goal go down to a competent Rangers side.

Alec "Eck" McNair was one of the stalwarts of Celtic during this season.

The war finished (or did it?) on Monday, 11 November, but one would not have thought so given the amount of casualties and illness that was so prevalent that foggy November. Celtic drew with Hearts on 9 November, were fogged off on 16 November, beat Partick Thistle narrowly 1–0 on 23 November, and then went down 1–3 to Motherwell at Fir Park on 7 December. Celtic were without Patsy Gallacher as well that day, and the *Daily Record* reports sadly and tellingly that Shaw, McNair and Cringan, all defenders, were the only players that "approached anything like Celtic class".

But then things took a turn for the better. On 14 December (coincidentally the day of the first ever general election in which women were allowed to vote in Great Britain), the Celtic crowd in the Grant Stand rose to their feet as a man at the sight of the great Napoleon running out of the pavilion, totally recovered. The return of the "Parkhead Foch" (Foch being the French General who was perceived as having won the war just ended!) made a huge difference as Celtic beat Dumbarton 2–0. McMenemy scored one goal and laid on the other for McColl. Also back that day for Celtic was Willie McStay, returned from war service, and soon after the New Year Celtic fans saw Joe Dodds return, and then Andy McAtee came back from service in the Italian Alps.

Two good victories came in December, and then on New Year's Day at Ibrox, Celtic earned an honourable draw against Rangers with McMenemy scoring for Celtic before Bowie equalised for Rangers. On a pleasant day, the crowd for the first peacetime meeting of the Old Firm was a massive 70,000, an enormous amount of them still wearing the "hospital blue" of injured soldiers as they were ushered into a special enclosure in front of the main stand. On a lighter note, some of the crowd were seen wearing captured German helmets!

The draw meant that Celtic were still in touch in the League race. They were five points behind, but had a game in hand, and as things gradually returned to some sort of normality, a League challenge was now a possibility. Slowly Celtic's forward line began to come together again into a recognisable McAtee, Gallacher, McColl, McMenemy and a new figure had appeared on the left wing called Adam McLean. He would turn out to be one of Celtic's best ever left wingers, and a half-back line now emerged of Willie McStay, Willie Cringan and Hugh Brown as Celtic began to come together again. The team did not again lose in the Scottish League that season – they drew twice against Motherwell at home and to Morton at Cappielow while Rangers stumbled, losing at Kilmarnock and beginning to draw games that they should have won.

Celtic's only defeat was to St Mirren in the one-off Victory Cup, brought in to take the place of the Scottish Cup – St Mirren would go on and win that trophy – but Patsy Gallacher now began to dominate games, and he had the men around him who could capitalise on his efforts. Andy McAtee, in particular, warmed the hearts of the crowd with some fine runs down the wing and crosses for Jimmy McColl to finish the job.

Soldiers now began to come back in greater numbers, sometimes to an uncertain future. Times had changed, and the loss of the German and the Russian markets was a serious blow for British industry as the country tried to regain some sort of economic composure, but for Celtic supporters, the month of April 1919 was a great one. On 12 April at Clydeholm Park, Clydebank, Jimmy McColl scored twice as Celtic beat the home side, while the press are unanimous in their praise for Eck McNair who broke up any Clydebank attack. But Rangers won that day as well, meaning that they were still three points ahead, but Celtic had two games in hand.

Next week was the Holiday Weekend and Celtic mopped up four points with Patsy Gallacher scoring a hat-trick against Falkirk and a couple against Airdrie. But Rangers also won their game on the Holiday Monday, and Celtic's next game was the following Monday, the Edinburgh Holiday for their visit to Tynecastle.

There had been overnight snow (on 28 April!) and it was still bitterly cold, but 15,000 were there to see a tight game where Celtic, having been in total command, were glad to hear the final whistle. They had scored twice through Jimmy McColl and once through Andy McAtee, but then near the end Andy Wilson who would become a legend for Scotland in a few years' time scored twice for Hearts, and Celtic were indebted to Shaw, McNair and Dodds for holding out at the end.

This meant that Celtic were now one point ahead of Rangers, and both teams had only one game left on 10 May. This was exceptionally late for 1919, but it was an exceptional season with Victory Internationals hastily arranged the previous Saturday. Celtic travelled to Ayr United while Rangers were at Clyde. Celtic only needed to beat Ayr for the Championship. The weather was pleasant and 10,000 were at Somerset Park with the trains from Glasgow all full. They saw a nervy display by Celtic for the first half hour but then good work from Patsy Gallacher found the unmarked Andy McAtee who shot home from the edge of the penalty box. The second half was long and painful with news coming through the public address system than Rangers were beating Clyde, but eventually with 10 minutes to go Adam McLean, now playing at centre-forward because McColl was injured, took up a pass from McAtee and scored.

The delight of the fans was tangible and obvious with Ayr Station that night seeing great scenes with 'The Wearing O' The Green' mingling incongruously with 'Pack Up Your Troubles' and 'It's a Long Way To Tipperary'. There had been no trouble that day, but the Ayr police were not sorry to see the trains depart, for Ireland was a tense place in 1919, and Celtic fans were aware of it all. They did now however have something to cheer about, as more and more soldiers came home to renew their acquaintance with Patsy Gallacher, Jimmy McMenemy, Eck McNair and Andy McAtee.

No other national trophies were competed for in 1919

CHAPTER 16

GLORY AT GREENOCK

1921/22

The early 1920s were difficult for all sorts of reasons. The general climate of economic and political uncertainty as Europe attempted to raise itself from its collective suicide attempt (now called the Great War) was bad enough; for the Celtic community, there were the additional effects of the struggle across the sea to establish a new country called Ireland. The times were tough.

On the other hand, it was also a time of social changes and advancement. More and more supporters now used motorised transport rather than the horse-driven "brake clubs" to go to away games, and were thus able to travel faster and further. The game was discussed in factories and written about in newspapers even more than before, as people used football (and the ever-thriving cinema) more and more to escape from the grim realities of 1920s life.

The Scottish League First Division now contained 22 clubs (generally reckoned to be too many) which necessitated 42 games. Celtic had lost out to Rangers in 1920 and 1921, and in what was reckoned as a welcome sign, the Scottish Cup in the first three years after the war was won by Kilmarnock, Partick Thistle (containing the old Celtic veteran Jimmy McMenemy) and Morton, three clubs who had never won the trophy before.

Celtic had disappointed their supporters in the last two years, but they had their great players. Patsy Gallacher was still there, now generally regarded to be the greatest of them all, and his skills up front had been supplemented by another, potentially even more talented, player called Tommy McInally who had now replaced the great Jimmy McMenemy. "The boy wonder", however, lacked the common sense that is so necessary if you want to be a footballer, and manager Maley would have his hands full with the Barrhead boy. The legendary defence of Shaw, McNair and Dodds were still there (Dodds having returned from an all-advised sojourn with Cowdenbeath), there was a strong half-back line of Gilchrist, Cringan and McMaster, and Andy McAtee and Adam McLean were still there on the wing, while there was a new centre-forward hero called Joe Cassidy, a man who had developed since the war.

The season started with a 4–0 defeat of Raith Rovers at Celtic Park, but there was a

Joe Cassidy.

disturbing tendency to draw games which they really should have won, something that was particularly true away from home. The away trip to Kirkcaldy was one such example, as indeed was a game at Pittodrie, and then on the Edinburgh Holiday Monday, they sustained their first defeat of the season to Hibs at Easter Road. That was in spite of a wonderful goal by Patsy Gallacher who received the ball from the centre after Hibs had scored a goal and dribbled his way through the defence to tap the ball past goalkeeper Harper.

The loss of the Glasgow Cup Final to Rangers was a blow, but it did not seem to do much to deter the astonishing amount of Celtic fanatics who would do anything to see their favourites. When they went to Dundee, for example, in October a dull 0–0 draw eventuated, but the *Dundee Courier* talks of men who walked all the way from Glasgow and back, and is surprised that those who arrived by the more conventional means of train or charabanc contained a "surprising amount of women and several small boy mascots dressed in the full Celtic outfit". They all departed Dundee "waving banners and emblems" to "accompaniment of weird noises from melodeons and bugles", some of them having stayed until the Sunday.

McInally scored a fine goal to earn a deserved point when Celtic visited Ibrox on 22 October, but away form continued to be disappointing. They were unlucky to lose 3–4 to Kilmarnock at Rugby Park but the draws at Motherwell and Ayr were miserable affairs. They did win an away game (for the first time since September) on Hogmanay at Hamilton but the effect was somewhat spoiled by the draws at the two New Year fixtures 0–0 at Celtic Park v. Rangers in a game that Celtic might have won, and a 1–1 draw against Clyde at Shawfield. Rangers were dropping points as well, but the League table after the New Year games showed Celtic still three points behind Rangers.

But Celtic now won three games in January, and another two in February, the only poor result being a disappointing goalless draw at Firhill. By the end of February, Celtic were three points ahead of Rangers in the League (Rangers had a game in hand) even though some of the performances continued to be disappointing. A devastating Scottish Cup exit to Hamilton Accies clearly lead to some tough talking from Mr Maley, and the following midweek in the League the result was reversed with Celtic winning 4–0 at Douglas Park. Ten games remained for both teams now, and Celtic had a two-point advantage.

It was round about now that Tommy McInally disappeared from the team. He may have been injured, but the fact that he was offloaded to Third Lanark at the end of the season makes one think that he was either simply dropped or had taken the huff with Maley. For whatever reason, the team never lost again that season, although there were two draws, again away from home at Third Lanark and Falkirk. It may have been the case that there was no room in the team for both McInally and Gallacher at the same time – certainly rumours circulated in the support that they did not get on – but there seemed little doubt that the team now prospered with Joe Cassidy in particular striking a rich seam of goals.

The absence of McInally also created an opportunity for a young man from Fife called John McFarlane. Called "Jean", presumably from the French Jean but maybe because of two cartoon characters in the *Weekly News* called "Jock and Jean", he would become a great left-half in years to come, but now he did not look at all out of place in a forward line of McAtee, Gallacher, Cassidy, McFarlane and McLean which at last began to function and score the goals – 4 against Dundee, 3 against Partick Thistle and 2 against Hearts in a significant away win at Tynecastle.

The end was exciting. On 15 April, when Morton were beating Rangers in the "roughest ever Scottish Cup Final", Celtic consolidated their position with a 2–0 win over Albion Rovers at Coatbridge, and then on the Holiday Monday, Patsy Gallacher scored twice and Joe Cassidy once to beat Partick Thistle. This mean that Celtic, with one game to play were five points ahead of Rangers who still had three to play. Rangers duly won their two games in hand, which meant that it all came down to the last day of the season, 29 April. Celtic were at Morton, and Rangers were at Clyde, and Celtic were a point ahead. Celtic had the better goal average, although there was some doubt in the minds of supporters about whether that would be the method used.

A bizarre incident happened on the Tuesday. Andy Cunningham of Rangers had been awarded a benefit, but was injured and could not play. While Andy walked out with the team, who took his place? None other than Patsy Gallacher! He was cheered by the Ibrox crowd for doing so, and it is maybe an indication that the rivalry in the 1920s was not quite so cutthroat as it is often portrayed.

It was tense at Greenock, though. The Morton crowd, still on a high after their Scottish Cup triumph, were not above "playing the Orange card" to antagonise the Celtic crowd, and on several occasions play had to be stopped for reasons of overcrowding at certain parts of the ground and sometimes sheer hooliganism. At half-time it looked possible that the game might have to be abandoned, but players of both sides helped usher the fans back onto the terracing. Morton were 1–0 up at half-time, and rumours were spreading that Rangers were hammering Clyde. The problem with "news" in the 1920s, however, was that it was often "made up" in the absence of modern accurate communications, and no one really knew. What they did know however was that Celtic had to grab at least a point, and preferably two.

They got one. Late in the game after some desperate attacking, Edwards the Morton goalkeeper could only palm a McFarlane drive out to the head of Andy McAtee. Five minutes remained, and everyone knew that a draw would not be enough, if indeed the score was 6–0 for Rangers at Shawfield, as the rumours said it was. The game at Morton finished 1–1, and as the sorely overstretched Greenock police ushered the Celtic fans to the train, no one knew for certain who the League champions were, although a wee boy claimed to have heard a newspaper reporter, who had phoned his office, say that it was 0–0 at Shawfield, and enough to give Celtic the title. Perhaps!

It was only when the trains pulled into Glasgow Central Station, and evening newspapers were on sale that it was confirmed that Celtic had won their sixteenth League title. Rangers had pressed and pressed but the brave Clyde defence had held out. Many Celtic supporters bought a drink for their Clyde supporting friends that night, as the joy knew no bounds.

Scottish Cup Final		
Morton 1 Rangers 0	Hampden	15 April
English Cup Final		
Huddersfield 1 Preston 0	Crystal Palace	29 April
English League		
Liverpool		

CHAPTER 17

McINALLY MAGIC

1925/26

The years from 1922 until 1925 had seen varied fortunes for Celtic. True, there had been two Scottish Cup victories, a competent one in 1923 and an epic one in 1925, but League form had been disappointing. Rangers won the League three times in a row, and for the first time since the turn of the century, it began to look as if Rangers' pre-eminence was going to last for a spell. Indeed, manager Struth had built up a fine team (although there was an Achilles heel in their failure to win the Scottish Cup since 1903) but in summer 1925 Celtic had reasons for confidence as well.

Their winning goal in the 1925 Scottish Cup Final had been scored by a young prodigy called James McGrory, a youngster who seemed to match all the striker's instincts along with broad shoulders and the ability to time a jump for a header. Two good players had emerged in the middle of the field. One was the boy from Beith in Ayrshire, Peter Wilson, commonly known as "Celtic's country bumpkin" after his unfamiliarity with Glasgow city life once saw him get lost in the Woolworth's

Celtic's great forward line of this season: Paddy Connolly, Alec Thomson, Jimmy McGrory, Tommy McInally, Adam McLean.

department store! He never got lost on the football field, though, and his visionary passing ability was a sight to behold. The other was inside-right Alec Thomson from Buckhaven in Fife. "Eckie Tamson" was a gritty hard-working character who was deceptively frail looking but was as tough as nails, could "fetch and carry" for McGrory, and could also take a goal himself.

And then, in summer 1925, Mr Maley took a bold step and brought back Tommy McInally, arguably the most talented ball player of the day. Tommy had fallen out with Celtic, basically because he lacked maturity, in 1922 and had spent the next three years in reluctant exile at Third Lanark. But Maley knew he was "pining for home" and, to the delight of the faithful, brought him back, hoping that he had now grown up.

For season 1925/26 at least, Maley's move was a pronounced success as Celtic won the Scottish League with a degree of ease. Rangers had a very poor season, finishing sixth, while Celtic's closest challengers were Airdrie and Hearts, but even they were eight points behind a Celtic team with whom no one could live over any length of time.

The Scottish League itself had seriously overreached. There were now three divisions. The snag about a Scottish League, however, is that it is just that and involved an awful lot of travelling including, for example, fixtures like Solway Star v. Brechin City. Teams simply could not afford the rail fares for that sort of thing, and one or two bankruptcies and a few others in serious financial problems in the difficult times of the 1920s led to the implosion of the third division in summer 1926, a problem in which Maley as League administrator would be heavily involved.

But Maley enjoyed consistent fortune with the Celtic team of 1925/26. He was particularly lucky in that he had very few injuries. There was a significant one to Adam McLean near the end of season, but apart from that, absences were few and far between and the team of Shevlin, W. McStay and Hilley; Wilson, J. McStay and McFarlane; Connolly, Thomson, McGrory, McInally and McLean more or less picked itself every week. And as with most good teams, they all got on together, looked out for each other, and were friendly off the field. People may jeer about concepts like "team spirit", but it is a *sine qua non* for any kind of sustained success on a football field. When it is absent, as it was two years later, disaster ensues.

Jimmy McGrory scored 35 League goals this season (almost one a game) and there was a spell between early November and mid-December when he scored at least one goal in seven successive games. The modest McGrory would himself say that between two talented inside forwards like Alec Thomson and Tommy McInally he simply had to score goals. He had no choice!

The season started well with five wins in a row until a complacent performance in the middle of September at the primitive Tannadice Park, home of Dundee United, brought things to a halt. Shortly after that, Maley made the mistake of bringing back the aged and not entirely fit Patsy Gallacher for a few games. This decision cost Celtic the Glasgow Cup, and also led to a most unusually large defeat 1–5 to the excellent Airdrie team which contained men like Bob McPhail and Hughie Gallacher. But Tommy McInally looked uninterested, and Patsy Gallacher did "little of note" in a Celtic performance which the *Sunday Post* describes as "inept".

Then Celtic lost 0–1 to Rangers at Ibrox on 17 October. It was an unlucky defeat with Celtic well on top in the second half and McInally having hard luck with two shots which hit the bar. It may have been a moral victory for Celtic, but they were nevertheless now sixth in the League table.

But it was as if someone had pressed a switch, and Celtic now went on a purple patch in which they never lost again until February. There were one or two draws, but generally the inside trio of Thomson, McGrory and McInally started to score the goals. Of the three, it was McInally who earned most plaudits. In a game against Raith Rovers at Stark's Park on 14 November, "none bettered McInally. Resourcefulness and cleverness stamped his every movement" and in a game against Hearts on 25 November, "the ball was manipulated with superb understanding" among Celtic's midfield four of Wilson, McFarlane, Thomson and McInally. By Hogmanay, in spite of a disappointing 1–1 draw on a snowbound pitch at Cowdenbeath, Celtic were top of the table.

The New Year's Day game at Celtic Park was a travesty. The game ended 2–2 but Celtic were all over them, McGrory scoring a trademark header in the third minute then McInally went through the Rangers defence "like a knife through cheese" to score a second. Unaccountably, Rangers then ran up and scored two goals and Celtic simply could not get a third. Yet it was a good result for Celtic, because the points divide meant an end to any realistic chance Rangers would have of getting back into the League race. McGrory then scored two against Queen's Park and a hat-trick against Partick Thistle as Celtic consolidated their position at the top. By 15 January, the *Dundee Courier* was predicting that the League title would go to Parkhead because none of their rivals had emerged as the single challenger, and they were all cutting each other's throats while Celtic marched on.

And march on Celtic did. There were one or two bad results – a draw at Hibs (albeit in an exciting 4–4 game) and a couple of narrow defeats at Kilmarnock and Motherwell – but the general pattern was progress in the Scottish League and the Scottish Cup with some fine results. A McGrory hat-trick against St Mirren on 9 March was much praised, and a 4–1 win over Aberdeen at the end of March put Celtic within touching distance of the League title.

But of course in 1926, it was the Scottish Cup that was considered to be of more importance, and Celtic were now in the final to be played on 10 April against St Mirren. This meant that the games on 3 April and 5 April were taken a little more gently than they should have been for fear of injuries being sustained. Thus, Kilmarnock at home and Partick Thistle away were goalless draws with McFarlane and McInally rested in the Holiday Monday game at Firhill. These draws were disappointments but they meant that Celtic now needed only two points for the title.

But if these games were disappointments, the Scottish Cup Final was a disaster. Celtic were without the injured Adam McLean, and playing in an unfamiliar white jersey, McInally and McGrory both had off days and the team never recovered from the loss of an early goal. Frankly, they had underestimated St Mirren whom they had trounced 6–1 in the League a month ago. It was Celtic's first Scottish Cup Final defeat since 1902, and was taken so badly by the support that only 3,000 were at Celtic Park on the following Wednesday to see the League title being clinched.

Morton scored first, but then goals by McGrory, McInally and Connolly saw Celtic through with a degree of ease to their seventeenth League title. Maley was happy, but admitted that the Scottish Cup Final was a crushing blow. But Celtic collected further silverware when they lifted the Glasgow Charity Cup in May just after the conclusion of the General Strike.

Scottish Cup Final		
St Mirren 2 Celtic 0	Hampden	10 April
English Cup Final		
Bolton Wanderers 1 Manchester City 0	Wembley	24 April
English League		
Huddersfield Town		

CHAPTER 18

McGRORY, McGRORY, HALLELUJAH!

1935/36

The late 1920s and early 1930s had not been happy years for Celtic. There had been some great moments, notably the Scottish Cup win over Motherwell and the American tour in 1931, but that had been overshadowed by the tragedy of John Thomson in 1931, and then Peter Scarff in 1933. On a more general note, this was the time of the economic depression and Celtic supporters were hit hard, and had less money to attend football matches, while Celtic themselves, although by no means poor, had incurred a huge expense in the construction of their new grandstand in 1929.

But in addition to all this, performances on the field were far from satisfactory with Rangers winning every Scottish League title between 1926 and 1936 with the exception of 1932, when Motherwell's excellent team of that era became champions instead. Thus, Celtic have Motherwell to thank for preventing Rangers doing nine-in-a-row long before Celtic did!

1934 and 1935 in particular were dreadful years. Maley, now in his late 60s and not easy to live with, kept beating on about the "Celts of old" and comparing the present team unfavourably with them, but seemed now to lack the drive to do anything about it. Those of us who lived through the early 1960s and early 1990s when Celtic refused to rise to the domination of Rangers will know exactly what life was like in the early 1930s!

It was not that there weren't good players at Celtic Park. It was simply that there was little leadership or guidance. But then Celtic appointed Jimmy "Napoleon" McMenemy as trainer. The job of trainer was, on the surface, a fairly menial one involving, mainly, the treatment of injured players and the organisation of running round the track at training sessions. In fact, Napoleon became de facto Assistant Manager (although he was never so-called and the humble McMenemy would have abhorred anything so pompous) and it was he more than Maley who was responsible for the great success of the later 1930s as Celtic recovered spectacularly.

C. Geatons, R. Hogg, J. Kennaway, J. Morrison, W. Buchan, G. Paterson
J. McMenemy, J. Delaney, J. M'Grory, W. Lyon, J. Crum, F. Murphy, W. Maley
Trainer Captain Manager

But the hero of the 1935/36 season was undeniably James Edward McGrory who scored 50 League goals, and not until Henrik Larsson in 2001 would we see such prolific scoring again. Yet, as McGrory would himself say, he could only score goals if the other members of the forward line did their job as well – and he had men of the calibre of Jimmy Delaney, Willie Buchan, Johnny Crum and Frank Murphy around him. A feature of that forward line, much encouraged by McMenemy, who himself played in a great forward line of 30 years previously, was the frequent interchanging of position with Delaney suddenly appearing on the left wing, for example, and McGrory himself on the right wing and Johnny Crum in the centre. Thanks to McMenemy's excellent training regime, the players were all superbly fit and could do this to perfection.

By 1935, the worst of the recession seemed to be past, and slowly, gradually things began to pick up. More and more goods began to be made, and more and more workers had money in their pockets wherewith to buy such goods. More importantly as far as Celtic were concerned, there was more money for railway travel and for admission to football matches.

The season started badly with a defeat at Pittodrie, a place where Celtic seldom did well. Indeed the black and golds of Aberdeen were to have themselves a great season, but the next League defeat was not to come until December. Celtic beat Rangers 2–1 at Ibrox in September (even without the injured McGrory) and the victory was due in no small measure to the saving of a penalty kick by Canadian goalkeeper Joe Kennaway, and some fine defensive work organised by captain Willie Lyon, the Englishman who had joined Celtic from Queen's Park.

The impression that this might be Celtic's year grew during the month of November when Celtic swept everyone aside (two successive 5–0 wins over Hibs and Arbroath, for example) and McGrory rampant. He beat Steve Bloomer's goalscoring record in October and then on 21 December in a 5–3 win over Aberdeen at Celtic Park he became the all-time best goalscorer when he beat the 362 scored by Hughie Ferguson

> "Midwinter gloom at Celtic Park
> December's frost hung hoary
> But you can keep your Santa Claus
> We've got James McGrory"

and this was after a curious result when they had gone down 0–1 to an incredulous Dunfermline at East End Park. It was a perfect bounce back.

The loss of the New Year's Day game to Rangers by 3–4 in the drenching rain at Celtic Park was not considered a great disaster, and the team came roaring back, beating St Johnstone, Queen of the South and Albion Rovers. But then, they hit a wobble, by losing to Hearts at Tynecastle and then, disastrously and unpredictably, to St Johnstone in the Scottish Cup.

It was then that Maley delivered a few stern words and McMenemy a few wise ones. Celtic were still in the best position to win the League. They were ahead of Rangers and three points behind Aberdeen, but had two games in hand. All Celtic had to do was win their remaining 11 games, none of them against their two main rivals. In any case, both Aberdeen and Rangers, still involved in the Scottish Cup, might "crack". But irrespective of all that, the destination of the Scottish League flag was all about Celtic, and both Maley and McMenemy agreed that if there was any doubt about what to do, give the ball to McGrory!

Celtic did indeed win all their remaining games, some of them with a bit of bother – narrow 3–2 wins at Queen's Park and Airdrie for example – but others gloriously, none more so than on 14 March when in a game against Motherwell at Parkhead, McGrory scored a hat-trick in less than three minutes!

"Wait a bit, don't be so fast
We've left the star turn to the last
There in the midst o' a' his glory
Goal a minute, James McGrory"

A week after that, Celtic got over a difficult hurdle at Dens Park, with Delaney and McGrory taking full advantage of two defensive errors, then Hibs were dispatched 4–1 with McGrory scoring again (incredibly, he was not chosen to play for Scotland against England at Wembley!) and then came the holiday weekend in which Celtic won both their games. The first one was away at Arbroath and was characterised by a diving header by McGrory amidst a ruck of legs to bullet home, and then at Celtic Park on the Monday, Celtic beat Clyde 2–1 not altogether convincingly, it has to be said, but goals by Frank Murphy and (inevitably) Jimmy McGrory saw them through.

The League was effectively won on the Saturday when Ayr United were beaten 6–0 at Celtic Park. Jimmy McGrory scored a hat-trick

"Tell me the old, old story
A hat-trick for McGrory!"

and even missed a penalty kick! Willie Lyon, Frank Murphy and Willie Buchan scored the others and this result meant that Celtic needed to lose their last game and Rangers to win their remaining three games by astronomical scores for the Championship to be lost. In the event, Rangers (who had won the Scottish Cup on the same day that Celtic beat Ayr United 6–0) drew in midweek, and by the time that Celtic went to Firhill on 25 April, they were the champions of Scotland for the first time since 1926.

It had been a hard-fought Championship, much cherished and celebrated by the faithful who now began to see the sunny uplands of hope after a decade of dreadful under-achievement. Maley revelled in the glory once more while the

James Edward McGrory.

more modest architects of the League winning – the three Jimmies, McMenemy, McGrory and Delaney – smiled happily, but typical of the men, stressed that it was a team performance.

Celtic also won the Glasgow Charity Cup this year (Delaney scoring a hat-trick in the final against Rangers), and the summer of 1936 was spent in glorious happiness. Trouble was however brewing in Spain, and that Hitler fellow in Germany was now beginning to look dangerous as well as foolish. And what were these silly rumours in the American magazines about the King and some wealthy American divorcee?

Scottish Cup Final		
Rangers 1 Third Lanark 0	Hampden	18 April
English Cup Final		
Arsenal 1 Sheffield United 0	Wembley	25 April
English League		
Sunderland		

CHAPTER 19

THE BEST IN BRITAIN

1937/38

In 1937 Celtic failed to repeat their success of 1936 in the Scottish League, but had more than ample compensation in the famous win in the Scottish Cup Final against Aberdeen on the occasion that Hampden held its record crowd – and those who were there insist that there was an awful lot more there than even the official crowd of 146,433!

In general, there was increasing despair about the world's inability to avoid another war. Already Spain was in the throes of a dreadful cataclysm, and it was not too difficult to work out that Hitler was now a major threat. Yet, there was also a determination to enjoy ourselves while we could. The Celtic team of this year would certainly entertain.

Season 1937/38 began none too impressively with among other things two defeats from Rangers (one in the Scottish League and one in the Glasgow Cup) and a particular shocker at Gayfield before an incredulous Arbroath crowd.

Celtic 1938. Back Row: Geatons, Hogg, Kennaway, Morrison, Crum, Paterson. Front Row: Delaney, MacDonald, Lyon, Divers, Murphy.

There were extenuating circumstances in the shape of injuries to Willie Lyon and Jimmy Delaney, but the team had not played at all well. Even as early as 9 October, things did not look any too bright for Celtic, now in sixth place in the League and heading nowhere.

But in that autumn of 1937, there were two departures, one of them inevitable and the other, on the surface a piece of money grubbing, but in fact a very astute piece of business. The inevitable one was the departure of the now ageing Jimmy McGrory who did not play again after the 4–3 win over Queen's Park on 16 October. He scored in that game but the *Glasgow Herald* is compelled to say with a hint of sadness "although his scheming was full of subtlety, his methods were inclined to hold up the attack".

In December, McGrory moved to become manager of Kilmarnock. His departure caused much pain, but it was a nostalgic kind of pain and realistic assessments concurred with the view that although Jimmy was still among the goals, this could not continue for much longer for he was now in his mid-30s, prone to injury and clearly slowing down. The affection for Jimmy McGrory, however, would remain for the rest of his life and beyond.

The other departure was a sudden one and apparently done without the consent of the player himself. Willie Buchan, the inside right suddenly found himself going to Blackpool for £10,000, an astonishing amount of money in 1937. The move did not immediately endear itself to the Celtic support, for Buchan was a good player, but it did at last give an opportunity for Malky MacDonald. MacDonald had been at Celtic Park for a few years now but had never been able to break into the side. He was a very versatile player, but it was his very versatility that prevented him being used as anything other than a "bits and pieces" player, deployed in the event of an injury. But now he settled into the inside right position of a devastating forward line which read Delaney, MacDonald, Crum, Divers and Murphy.

From 27 November until 19 March, the team never dropped a League point. Even injuries to key men like Jimmy Delaney and Chick Geatons were coped with, for there were adequate replacements in Joe Carruth and Matt Lynch. In December, an excellent 3–0 win at Easter Road over Hibs was followed by an 8–0 thumping of Kilmarnock at Celtic Park on Christmas Day. This was McGrory's first game as manager of Kilmarnock, and although he was no stranger to goals raining in at Celtic Park, this must have been a horrible start for him, with a certain amount of evidence that Maley enjoyed McGrory's discomfiture, and a hint perhaps that McGrory's departure had not been as amicable as it might have been.

There then followed the famous game on New Year's Day 1938 at Celtic Park. 92,000 is given as the attendance and this is claimed to be the record crowd for the ground. Certainly there are reports of gross overcrowding and gates having to be closed, and the on-the-field action was impressive as well. John Divers scored twice and Malky MacDonald once (with a penalty) as Celtic crushed Rangers 3–0, but the man who was singled out by the press for his contribution was Johnny Crum, now having taken over the mantle of McGrory as centre-forward. He didn't score but led the line well, distributing the ball to wingers Carruth and Murphy with ease and a touch of arrogance, and himself roaming about from wing to wing. Willie Lyon was described as "impassable" in the centre of the defence and in Rangers' only real attempt at goal, Joe Kennaway "brought the house down" with a great save from a McPhail drive.

All this meant that Celtic were now at the top of the League with a surprise challenge this year coming from Hearts. By sheer luck, Hearts were next on the fixture list on 8 January at Tynecastle and Celtic's 4–2 win over them (with Crum and Divers scoring two each) before a 42,000 crowd more or less, even at this early stage, ensured that Celtic were the favourites to win the League. Hearts were leading 2–1 until late in the game when Johnny Crum "almost impudent in his daring" took control and saw Celtic home in one of the many good games played between Hearts and Celtic at Tynecastle over the years.

Aberdeen were then dispatched 5–2, Clyde 6–1 and Arbroath 4–0 before a tight game at Muirton Park, Perth on 19 February saw Celtic edge home 2–1, then came an impressive 5–1 beating of St Mirren at Celtic Park at the end of the month.

March, however, saw a stumble. There was the disastrous loss of the Scottish Cup quarter-final to Kilmarnock, after which Maley, clearly forgetting his own dictum of "it is our proud boast that we can taste the fruits of victory in the same way as the bitterness of defeat" went out of his way to snub Jimmy McGrory, and then a couple of disappointing home draws were followed by a 3–0 defeat at Brockville on 2 April. This run clearly imperilled Celtic's chances of winning the League, but they were still marginally ahead of Hearts by a point and a game in hand as they approached their final six fixtures.

Celtic beat Motherwell 4–1 at Celtic Park on 9 April, and this was followed by a double-header against Dundee over the Holiday Weekend. The Saturday game at Dens Park was a tight 3–2 victory with two goals from John Divers and one from Joe Carruth, and some good defensive work by Willie Lyon after Dundee scored with a penalty late in the second half to make it 3–2, but the game at Parkhead on the Monday was more one-sided. Celtic won this one 3–0. It was a game spoiled to an extent by "over-robust" Dundee defending (clearly there were some vendettas carried over from Saturday) but Willie Lyon scored with two penalties and John Divers scored the other goal.

The *Dundee Courier* admitted that there were no "angels in paradise" that day, but all this meant that Celtic only needed a point from their two remaining games against St Mirren and Hibs to win the League. On 23 April, they travelled to Love Street and won 3–1. It was actually a fine game of football. Crum scored in the first minute, Delaney added a second, then after St Mirren pulled one back before half-time Crum scored in the second half to delight the travelling fans in the large crowd. It was the same day as the Scottish Cup Final between East Fife and Jimmy McGrory's Kilmarnock which ended in a 1–1 draw.

Celtic were worthy champions and their summer of 1938 got even better when they won both the Glasgow Charity Cup, beating Rangers 2–0 in the Final, and then of course the all-British Empire Exhibition Trophy. John Divers, in particular, had come good just at the right time, but in truth, it was a great Celtic side, and 1938 was a fine year to celebrate the 50 years of the club's existence.

Scottish Cup Final		
East Fife 4 Kilmarnock 2	Hampden	27 April
(after 1-1 draw at Hampden on 23 April)		
English Cup Final		
Preston North End 1 Huddersfield 0	Wembley	30 April
English League		
Arsenal		

CHAPTER 20

ISOLATED BUT WELCOME

1953/54

Even though there had a been a terrible war which had knocked out all official football between seasons 1939/40 and 1945/46, 1938, the last time that Celtic had won the League was a long time ago. The truth was, however, that Celtic had not even come close. It was barely comprehensible that a club which still retained its massive support had been so abominably bad since the war years. The 1940s remain a Celtic horror story and it was not until 1951 that Celtic actually won a national trophy – the Scottish Cup in 1951.

In the Scottish League, the only real challengers to Rangers had been Hibs. They had a good side, notably the Famous Five forward line of Smith, Johnstone, Reilly, Turnbull and Ormond, and so good had they been that some Celtic supporters had almost threatened to transfer allegiance totally to them on the grounds that Hibs, and only Hibs, seemed capable of offering a challenge to Rangers.

Yet in summer 1953, Celtic had staggered the footballing world by winning the Coronation Cup, an all-British tournament to commemorate the arrival to the throne of Queen Elizabeth II. They had beaten Hibs in the Final. There were clearly players of ability as Celtic Park, and it was just really a question of whether they could be moulded together into a team which could produce the consistency to win the Scottish League.

The Scottish League Cup of 1953/54 was predictably miserable for Celtic, the Glasgow Cup was worse, and the early part of the League campaign was full of inconsistent performances, although there was a clear difference between home form and away form. Home games tended to be won comfortably (3–0 v. Aberdeen and Raith Rovers, 2–0 v. Hearts, 4–1 v. Airdrie and 4–0 v. St Mirren) whereas when out of sight of the Gallowgate and Parkhead Cross, homesickness tended to set in and there had been some shockers of results at Queen of the South, Stirling Albion and East Fife. Little wonder, perhaps, that the support sometimes turned awful at provincial venues, and many respectable Scottish towns would view the arrival of the green and white hordes in the same vein as medieval villages viewed the imminence of the Black Death.

The League was small at this time – only 16 teams and therefore 30 games – but the saving grace for Celtic was that everyone else was similarly inconsistent,

The programme cover for the game which won the League for Celtic at Easter Road for the first time in 16 years.

Rangers possibly even more so than Celtic, and no one strong team had risen to dominate proceedings. Celtic had a good Boxing Day beating neighbours Clyde 7–1 at Shawfield with Neil Mochan, John Higgins and Bobby Collins all scoring two each, but that only raised them to fourth place behind surprise leaders Queen of the South, then Dundee and Hearts. Rangers were in mid-table obscurity and Hibs not all that far away from the relegation zone. It was a strange League table, but it meant that the destination of the flag was very open.

Celtic's inconsistency continued in January 1954. New Year's Day saw a low-key 1–0 win over Rangers at Celtic Park and other wins over Falkirk and Queen of the South at home, but there was also a defeat at Pittodrie and on 6 February, Celtic lost at Tynecastle. It was a last-minute goal unbelievably allowed by referee Barclay of Kirkcaldy for what looked to the press and Celtic fans as an illegal use of the elbow by Jimmy Wardhaugh in what should have been a "shoulder charge" on Celtic's goalkeeper George "Sonny" Hunter. It did little to soothe the Celtic paranoia complex, but it meant that Celtic were now seven points behind Hearts, admittedly with games in hand – but they did not really look like winning them!

But then, suddenly, it all began to click for Celtic. The team became more settled, and did all that they needed to do to take over at the top – win games! The half-back line of Bobby Evans, Jock Stein and Bertie Peacock suddenly took command of the midfield, the left-wing partnership of Charlie Tully and Neil Mochan suddenly sparked into action, and the deployment of Sean Fallon in the centre-forward position (not on the face of it a promising move, for Sean was a rugged full-back who could not replace Mike Haughney or Frank Meechan) suddenly worked, with Fallon getting himself on the score sheet quite a lot. Goalkeeper John Bonnar had been out injured for a spell, but his return further stabilised the defence.

But possibly the greatest contribution was made by Willie Fernie, whose dribbling and passing skills now came to the fore. He teamed up well with winger John Higgins and very soon the right wing was as good as the left. Charlie Tully was sometimes an enigma. He was certainly very talented but like quite a few showmen before and after, Charlie could never resist playing to the gallery, and sometime his team mates could show exasperation when a chance for a goal was lost while Charlie entertained his large fan club.

The big difference came in the away form. The team who could hardly win away from home suddenly began to do so, winning at Airdrie 6–0 one Wednesday afternoon in the middle of March and then following it up with a win at Partick Thistle on the Saturday. The game at Broomfield was an excellent example of the way Celtic had upped a gear this spring with Neil Mochan scoring a hat-trick, and the Saturday game saw a few of Fallon's doubters silenced when the Irishman scored twice to rout Thistle.

Progress was also made in the Scottish Cup and after the defeat of Motherwell (then in the Second Division) in a replay of the semi-final on the Holiday Monday, attention was turned to the Scottish League. It was ironic that the team "which couldn't win away games" now won the Scottish League by doing just that. First up was St Mirren where 18,000 (huge for an early evening Wednesday kick-off) saw a tight game which Celtic won 3–1. They were uninspiring but competent, exactly what is required to win League Championships with goals from Charlie Tully, Bobby Collins and a Mike Haughney penalty. This win now meant that Celtic were now one point ahead of Hearts and a game in hand with only three matches left.

Neither Celtic nor Hearts played on the Saturday, but Rangers did in the Scottish Cup semi-final and managed to lose 0–6 to Aberdeen, in what seemed like a protest by the players at the aged and increasingly tyrannical Bill Struth. However much Celtic fans may have enjoyed that, they themselves had not won anything yet, and on Wednesday, 14 April, Celtic went to the extremely dangerous ground of Brockville, Falkirk.

This was a far more assured Celtic performance, and they won 3–0 to put themselves within touching distance of the flag. 22,000 saw a goal from Fallon, and then two from Neil Mochan as the half-back line of Evans, Stein and Peacock kept a stranglehold on the game to the delight of the Celtic fans. Brockville in the 1950s was almost a byword for poor Celtic performances, overcrowding and bad behaviour, but this was one of the happier occasions. Celtic now only had to win at either Easter Road on the Saturday or Hamilton at home to assure themselves of the Championship.

Easter Road was heaving with well over 45,000 inside as Neil Mochan scored in 90 seconds to set Celtic on their way. To their credit, a depleted Hibs side without Gordon Smith and Laurie Reilly fought back, but although they enjoyed a fair amount of territorial possession, Celtic remained in control, Neil Mochan scored again and then with only minutes remaining, Johnny Higgins headed home a Willie Fernie cross to guarantee the flag as Celtic won 3–0.

Edinburgh belonged to Celtic that night, as they celebrated long and hard. The following week they won the Scottish Cup as well, beating Aberdeen 2–1. 1954 was a great year for Celtic and their long-suffering supporters.

Scottish Cup Final		
Celtic 2 Aberdeen 1	Hampden	24 April
Scottish League Cup Final		
East Fife 3 Partick Thistle 2	Hampden	24 October
English Cup Final		
West Bromwich Albion 3 Preston 2	Wembley	1 May
English League		
Wolverhampton Wanderers		

CHAPTER 21

RELIEF BEYOND BELIEF

1965/66

John Divers could never have guessed what he was starting when he scored the opening goal for Celtic at Tannadice Park on Wednesday, 25 August 1965. Not only was it the first goal in a 4–0 thumping of Dundee United in the first League game of the season (Joe McBride, Tommy Gemmell and Ian Young got the others), a victory that was all the sweeter after some indifferent form in the League Cup, but it was in fact the first goal of Celtic's nine-in-a-row League titles from 1965/66 until 1973/74.

Summer 1965 had been euphoric. The return of Jock Stein as manager and the capture of the Scottish Cup in April had triggered an explosion of joy which had not been seen for many years. Not only that, but there was anticipation of the good things to come. No one could have anticipated just how good things were going to be, but in any case there was a great deal of hard work to be done.

Jock Stein made no bones about it. His priority was winning the Scottish League. It had not been won since Stein himself had been the captain in 1954, and before that the previous success had been 1938. For a club of Celtic's stature, tradition and support, this was frankly unacceptable, and for this reason, although some success in Europe would be nice as indeed would be the capturing of the two Scottish domestic trophies, the main priority was the recapture of the Scottish League flag which had been absent from Celtic Park for so long.

Stein was also at pains to insist through the new organ *The Celtic View* and other sources that the League was not normally won on a gloriously romantic occasion at Hampden in the spring sunshine. It was more about "flint hard pitches at Kilmarnock in December" and "heavy boggy pitches at Falkirk in February", and the winning of the League demanded character as well as flair. The good thing of course was that a League campaign of 34 games did allow a few "second chances". Unlike the Scottish Cup, for example, you were allowed the occasional defeat. This was just as well in 1965/66!

Having defeated Clyde unconvincingly on 11 September, the team sustained its first reverse of the season at Ibrox. It was only 1–2 and there was an excuse that Billy McNeill was injured, but it did mean that for the moment Rangers had their noses in front. It was only a temporary setback, however, for good home wins against Aberdeen and Hearts followed with loads of goals. In the midst of all that, Stein managed to upset Rangers by claiming that their floodlights

Bobby Lennox scores at Motherwell on the day that Celtic won the League in May.

were sub-standard for a League Cup semi-final!

The League Cup was won in late October when John Hughes scored with his two penalties to beat Rangers, but as significant as anything for Celtic's Scottish League campaign were the two victories on either side of this game – vital and hard-fought away victories at Falkirk (a thrilling 4–3 affair) and at Dundee on the Wednesday night after the Hampden triumph, when in spite of some late Dundee pressure, Celtic held on for a 2–1 victory.

There was a certain amount of satisfaction among the support about the way in which games were being won. The accent was on attacking football and clearly Joe McBride had been a great success since arriving from Motherwell, but there was also sensible defending, and a new professionalism about the team who realised that games simply had to be won. But the thought that the Scottish League Cup was already at Celtic Park this season, and that the Scottish Cup was still there from last season was a great stimulus and comfort for both the players and the supporters.

The campaign up to Christmas was a good one with wins over St Johnstone at Perth (where the record had previously been poor) and crucially at Dunfermline the week before Christmas, hard on the heels of another good win against Hibs at Parkhead. Christmas Day itself was a remarkable 8–1 defeat of Morton. It was one of those games where you simply did not want the referee to blow his final whistle.

Even better came on 3 January, when Rangers were put to the sword to the tune of 5–1 in the fog and the frost of Parkhead. This had followed a win at Shawfield (a ground where Celtic seemed to draw depressingly often) and on the second Saturday of the year a Charlie Gallagher goal was enough to beat Dundee United.

Things were looking lovely for Celtic, but then, as was always likely to happen, the team hit a bad patch. The games against Dinamo Kiev in Europe meant perhaps that Celtic took their eye off the ball as far as Scottish League games were concerned, as defeats were sustained at Pittodrie and Tynecastle. The Tynecastle game should never have been played for Celtic only arrived back from the Soviet Union late on the Friday night, and the Pittodrie game was played on a very hard pitch, but the net result of all this meant that at the end of January, Rangers had clawed back the lead that Celtic had established by their 5–1 victory and that the teams were level on points.

This was not in itself disastrous but then there was a further reverse at the end of February at the old bogey ground of Stirling Albion, and things looked grim. But progress was made in other trophies, and on the night that Celtic beat Hearts in the Scottish Cup quarter-final, Rangers went down 2–3 to Falkirk at Brockville. Then on Monday, 21 March, Celtic supporters left Firhill disappointed with their team's 2–2 draw with Partick Thistle but their disappointment changed to joy when they heard that Dundee United had beaten Rangers.

Other tournaments now played a part. In between Celtic's games against Liverpool in the European Cup-winners' Cup, Celtic travelled to Hibs in

Celebrations can be dangerous for these lads on the roof! Ronnie Simpson looks a little precarious as well!

unseasonable snowy weather on 16 April but disappointed their fans with a 0–0 draw, allowing Rangers to narrow the gap to only two points.

It is certainly true to say that Celtic were unlucky to lose to both Liverpool and Rangers in the Cup-winners' Cup and the Scottish Cup Final, but unlucky or not, Celtic now had to reckon with the possibility of losing the Scottish League as well. They had three games left. They were two points ahead of Rangers, had a game in hand and a superior goal average, but any mistake could change all that. The remaining games were against Morton at Cappielow, Dunfermline at Celtic Park and Motherwell at Fir Park, whereas Rangers had to travel to Dunfermline and then Clyde at Ibrox.

The vital game was at Morton on 30 April, only a few days after the depressing Scottish Cup Final defeat. Celtic found themselves up against a team battling relegation and containing old Celtic warhorse Jim Kennedy in their ranks. In the first half, Morton missed a penalty kick which would have made all the difference, but then the "likely lads" of Jimmy Johnstone and Bobby Lennox scored to allow Celtic to edge home and relegate Morton. Rangers meanwhile kept the Championship alive by beating Dunfermline at East End Park.

Effectively it was Wednesday, 4 May which decided matters. It was tense at Celtic

Scottish Cup Final		
Rangers 1 Celtic 0	Hampden	27 April
(after 0-0 draw at Hampden on 23 April)		
Scottish League Cup Final		
Celtic 2 Rangers 1	Hampden	23 October
English Cup Final		
Everton 3 Sheffield Wed 2	Wembley	14 May
English League Cup Final		
West Bromwich Albion 5 West Ham United 3		
(played on a home and home basis)		
English League		
Liverpool		

Park. While Rangers were beating Clyde comprehensively 4–0, Alex Ferguson scored for Dunfermline with a curious half-hit trundler, and that was how it stood at half-time. But once again the "likely lads" turned up trumps to win the game 2–1. All this meant that Celtic were more or less there – as long as they didn't lose 4–1 to Motherwell at Fir Park on Saturday. Jock Stein refused to celebrate, although the *Evening Times* reported that "there wasn't a dry eye in the house".

The sun shone both literally and metaphorically at Fir Park on Saturday, 7 May. Rangers had conceded and congratulated on the Thursday morning, for Celtic were not really likely to concede four goals to a Motherwell team which had given up for the season. In the event it was really rather a dull game enlivened only by Bobby Lennox scoring in the last minute. After 12 long years, Celtic were once again the champions of Scotland.

CHAPTER 22

ON THE ROAD TO LISBON

1966/67

1967 is, of course, rightly famed for mighty deeds on the European stage, and one often feels that there is a danger of underestimating what happened on the domestic scene. Both domestic cups were won (and the venerable Glasgow Cup as well) and the Scottish League was won for the second year in a row. Celtic had not won the Scottish League two years in a row since the long ago days of the First World War, when they won it in 1916 and 1917.

It is important too to realise that the opposition was not negligible – a charge that has frequently been laid in other seasons by those who enjoy sneering at Scottish football. 1967 was, in fact, one of the better seasons in Rangers' history. True, they won nothing and they had their grizzly horror show at Berwick in the Scottish Cup, but they did reach the Final of a major European trophy (and were considered unlucky to lose it). They were also arguably the better team in the Scottish League Cup Final against Celtic in October. But the very fact that they managed to stay with the Lisbon Lions for so long is itself an indication that they were no bad side. Rangers have had many worse sides who have actually won things!

In addition, Kilmarnock reached the semi-final of what is now known as the Europa League, and Aberdeen, Dunfermline, both Dundee teams were respectable outfits with even the two chronic underachievers of Edinburgh capable of one or two good moments. Scottish football, albeit still smarting from the pain of having watched England win the World Cup the previous summer, was in good heart.

But it soon became obvious that no one could live with Celtic. Having

Jimmy Johnstone in full flow.

romped through their League Cup section, they had an important early success in September when they beat Rangers 2–0 at Celtic Park, both goals coming early from Bobby Murdoch and Bertie Auld, the men who would prove to be the mainstays of that excellent team. By the end of October, not only had the League Cup been won, but in the Scottish League Celtic had not dropped a single point.

Much of the success had been due to their summer tour of the USA and Canada. It had been a tremendous bonding experience. Not all tours are successes. There are frequent cliques, arguments, disputes, bad behaviour, tantrums, sulkings and sendings home. Not this one, however. Jock Stein was at the peak of his powers, made sure that the team played well and brought it about that the team "bonded" into a cohesive unit of very fit and very enthusiastic young men. It was also very much in the Celtic tradition of Maley using Seamill Hydro and other places for such purposes.

Eventually, in early November, they dropped a point to St Mirren at Celtic Park. Even then, there were extenuating circumstances in that Billy McNeill was out with flu and Bobby Murdoch was sent off (possibly in a case of mistaken identity), but Celtic dropping a point caused quite a stir this season. They were frequently compared to Perry Mason, the lawyer star of an American soap opera who always won his case. It was usually shown on BBC on a Saturday night before the football programme and the question was asked: "Who is going to lose first? Celtic or Perry Mason?"

There were only another two points dropped between early November and Christmas. One was on a hard pitch at Kilmarnock, a result whose effects were mitigated because Rangers went down to Dunfermline that day, and then on Christmas Eve at Pittodrie both teams seemed to underperform and the game ended 1–1.

That was the game in which Joe McBride sustained the injury which ended his season, but as far as Celtic were concerned, it didn't matter all that much for they had already signed Willie Wallace from Hearts. To the delight of the *Sunday Post*, the Celtic fans had a banner saying "Oor Wullie" on his debut, and this signing was a major coup for Jock Stein and his increasingly impressive and apparently unbeatable Celtic side.

But they did lose on New Year's Eve at Tannadice Park, Dundee. Goalkeeper Ronnie Simpson had one of his very few bad games, but Jock immediately spotted another problem and changed things. The full-back partnership had been Gemmell and O'Neill since the tour of the USA, but this meant no place for Jim Craig. In addition, Gemmell was better on the left than on the right, so after the New Year the full-back partnership became Craig and Gemmell.

Frost meant the postponement of the New Year fixture between Rangers and Celtic, but otherwise in what was a fairly mild winter, all the other games went ahead with progress made in all competitions until another slight spoke was put in the wheel of the Celtic bandwagon – and this was from our old enemies of Stirling

Albion who managed a draw at the end of February when possibly Celtic were concentrating on the imminence of the European Cup quarter-final in Vojvodina. Dunfermline then put up a hard fight again at Celtic Park but Celtic just got the better of them by 3–2 (the game at East End Park in November had been an unbelievably thrilling 5–4) and then Falkirk, Hearts and Partick Thistle were put to the sword in quick succession.

Then between the home and away legs of the Dukla Prague semi-final, and with the country on a huge high following the win over England at Wembley, Celtic dropped another point (Shock! Horror!) to Aberdeen in a very dull goalless draw at Celtic Park. Both teams were thinking of other things, for in addition to the European Cup commitment, these two teams were due to meet in the Scottish Cup Final and the word "rehearsal" was bandied about in the press. Rehearsals are rarely entertaining, and this one was no exception. It may be true, however, as some claimed, that Jock Stein was using this game as "defensive practice" for Dukla Prague. Very seldom do Celtic play two goalless draws back to back!

As Celtic fans celebrated the Scottish Cup victory against Aberdeen on 29 April, a rumour spread round the Celtic end that we had won the League as well because Dundee had beaten Rangers. This was not quite true, for the result at Dens Park had been 1–1, but it did mean that Celtic only had to beat Dundee United on Wednesday night at Parkhead to be crowned champions. Failing that, there was Rangers at Ibrox on the Saturday (where a draw would suffice) and if all that failed, there was another game against Kilmarnock.

The game against Dundee United saw a huge triumphant Celtic crowd, still basking in their Scottish Cup triumph. There was a certain arrogance in the crowd and some complacency among the players, and Dundee United, to the amazement of their own shell-shocked supporters, beat Celtic for the first time ever at Celtic Park.

Scottish Cup Final		
Celtic 2 Aberdeen 0	Hampden	29 April
Scottish League Cup Final		
Celtic 1 Rangers 0	Hampden	29 October
European Cup Final		
Celtic 2 Inter Milan 1	Lisbon	25 May
English Cup Final		
Tottenham Hotspur 2 Chelsea 1	Wembley	20 May
English League Cup Final		
Queens Park Rangers 3 West Bromwich Albion 2	Wembley	4 March
English League		
Manchester United		

Naturally the conspiracy theorists had a field day about this one for it gave Celtic the chance to win the League at Ibrox against Rangers. It seemed to be a reasonable "game plan". That idea does less than credit to a good Dundee United team who had now beaten Celtic twice this season, but there is little doubt that the result made for good "box office" at Ibrox and loads of world media attention, including one Helenio Herrera of Inter Milan.

The rain was incessant and thunderstorms were not far away as both teams, now in European finals, battled it out. It was a remarkably even and symmetrical game which ended 2–2 with one good goal and one scrappy one for each side. Jimmy Johnstone it was who scored Celtic's two goals, and the 2–2 result was good enough to earn Celtic their 22nd League title. It also proved that although Rangers won nothing that season, they were nevertheless good enough to stay with Celtic.

There was also another game in Lisbon that summer…

CHAPTER 23

MAKING THEM CRACK!

1967/68

Everyone knew, as season 1967/68 kicked off, that it was going to be difficult to follow the 1967 European Cup season. No one could imagine just how difficult it was going to be, but the ability of the team and the manager to bounce back from the disasters of the early season was a mark of just how good they were. In some ways 1968 was as much of a triumph as 1967 had been – less spectacular, obviously, but just as rewarding for the players and the supporters.

Summer 1967 had been one long bask in glory. Jock Stein possibly may have made a mistake by not making any new major signings to his squad. A new face or two – and everyone would have now wanted to join this club – might have added a little spice to things and introduced an element of competition for places, but on the other hand it was difficult to argue that the team that had just won the European Cup needed any additions. Perhaps, however, standing still is never the best option.

Certainly complacency crept in, and it was a shame to see such talent failing to live up to the now mega high expectations. By the end of January 1968, Celtic were in a considerable amount of trouble. The only real plus point was the fact that the Scottish League Cup was back on the sideboard. It had been won in a high-scoring and highly entertaining Final against Dundee in late October, and that had followed the breath taking defeat of Rangers at the sectional stage and then an electrifying 7–1 defeat of Morton in the semi.

On the other hand, two major disasters had been sustained on the European and International front. They had gone out of the European Cup at the first time of asking, the damage done in the first leg at Parkhead in a lacklustre performance against Dinamo Kiev which had been so disappointing to the fans. Worse came in the South American fiasco which, on reflection, they would have been better out of, and from which they certainly should have come home before that awful deciding match in Montevideo. They lost more than a chance to become the World Champions that day; they lost their reputation for good behaviour as well.

By Christmas there was a certain steadying of the situation and the feeling that things were improving, but then two blows came our way in January. On 2 January at Celtic Park, Celtic were well on top of Rangers and really should have won comfortably until two goalkeeping errors gave Rangers an undeserved draw and allowed the Ibrox men to maintain their lead at the top of the League. (They had won the game at Ibrox in September.) Worse came at the end of January when the team, admittedly without Craig, Clark and Auld, went out of the Scottish

Charlie Gallagher, whose moment of glory this was.

Cup to Dunfermline Athletic at Celtic Park in a game where the supporters quite simply had to raise their hands and admit that the Pars were the better side.

This left Celtic with only the League to play for. Well no, that is not correct, for there was also the Glasgow Cup which, often despised and rejected in the 1960s, nevertheless played a vital part in the winning of the Scottish League, as we shall see. But at the beginning of February, things looked bleak as far as the League was concerned, mainly because it was out of Celtic's hands. Teams played each other only twice in those days and there were no Old Firm fixtures left – at least in the League.

But there was still Jock Stein, the master tactician and player of mind games. Jock realised that Rangers with an inexperienced manager called Davie White (a man who had done very well with Clyde and would do well with Dundee in the future, but the job at Ibrox was just too much for him) could crack under pressure. Stein's encouragement to his team (still very talented in spite of this season's reverses) was to go out and play attacking football. This would have three benefits, he felt. One was that it would boost the goal average (and it might come down to that), another was that it would put the pressure on Rangers if they saw that Celtic were winning all their games comfortably) and a third was that Celtic's attacking style of play would win round the press and neutral opinion. After all, even Celtic's enemies agreed that a winning Celtic side, playing with style and panache, was very attractive to watch.

An injury to Bertie Auld necessitated the introduction of Charlie Gallagher, the quiet man of Parkhead but whose moment of glory this was – "cometh the hour, cometh the man" – and also Jim Brogan was brought in to replace John Clark. There was little wrong with Clark, but Brogan was just a little more aggressive and attack-minded. Results now began to follow, and eyebrows were raised with a very impressive 6–0 defeat of Kilmarnock on a heavily sanded Rugby Park pitch in early March.

It was then that the first crack in the Rangers edifice became apparent. They were due to play Celtic in the Glasgow Cup, but suddenly announced that they were withdrawing from the tournament! Their argument was that they were involved in Europe and the Scottish Cup as well as the Scottish League and they were worried about fixture congestion, etc. but to the Scottish footballing public at large, this seemed like cowardice as well as an insult to a competition which was older than the Scottish League! Stein and Celtic retained a dignified silence and allowed Rangers to score that own goal – but the press turned on Rangers, and even their own supporters were unhappy about this. They even said that Rangers were now the IRA club of Glasgow, the letters standing for I Ran Away!

In the meantime, Celtic absolutely piled on the pressure with great away wins at St Johnstone, Dundee United, Hearts and Aberdeen while Rangers struggled. Hearts put them out of the Scottish Cup and Leeds United put them out of Europe, and then in early April they dropped a point to Dundee United at Tannadice

Friendly rivals. Roy Barry of Dunfermline Athletic and Billy McNeill of Celtic before the start of the game which confirmed Celtic as champions on 30 April 1968. Roy Barry is carrying the Scottish Cup which his team won the previous Saturday

There was now only one point in it, and Celtic now had a far better goal average.

It all went Celtic's way on Wednesday, 17 April. When Celtic were winning the Glasgow Cup (yes, the Glasgow Cup which Rangers ran away from) by beating Clyde 8–0, Rangers, behind at one point, fought back to earn a draw at Morton – but it was only a draw and Celtic were now top of the League on goal average. But Morton still had to come to Celtic Park the following Saturday, and they held out until the very last minute before a goal came off Bobby Lennox's shin to release bedlam at Celtic Park.

Rangers, psyched out and outmanoeuvred, then blew up completely by losing their last game of the season to Aberdeen at Ibrox. They had insisted on playing that game in competition to the Scottish Cup Final between Dunfermline and Hearts, thus insulting the Scottish Cup as well as the Glasgow Cup, and once again were railed at in the press for their arrogance. They duly paid the penalty for that. The idea that Rangers ran Scottish football died hard at Ibrox.

Scottish Cup Final		
Dunfermline 3 Hearts 1	Hampden	27 April
Scottish League Cup Final		
Celtic 5 Dundee 3	Hampden	28 October
English Cup Final		
West Bromwich Albion 1 Everton 0	Wembley	18 May
English League Cup Final		
Leeds United 1 Arsenal 0	Wembley	2 March
English League		
Manchester City		

Celtic had now effectively won the League unless they went down by something like 16–0 to Dunfermline on Wednesday night. That never happened, for Celtic won 2–1 at a dangerously over crowded East End Park in what was a carnival atmosphere of the Scottish League winners v. the Scottish Cup winners. These two clubs had always had a good relationship with each other, and how they all enjoyed Dunfermline coming out with the Scottish Cup, and Jock Stein trying to steal the Cup from George Farm!

Of all Celtic's Scottish League triumphs, this one must rank very highly. It combined excellent play with the character to bounce back from adversity, and the added spice at the end was that neutral opinion agreed with Celtic supporters that justice had been done.

Celtic 1969.

Three domestic trophies won in 1969. Players are Tommy Callaghan, Willie Wallace, Bertie Auld and John Clark.

Celebrating in the Easter Road dressing room in April 1977.

Joe Craig in 1977. Better get rid of that bottle before big Jock comes in and sees it!

Billy McNeill, captain of all nine of Celtic's "9 in a row".

Danny McGrain.

Roy Aitken.

Tommy Craig and Billy McNeill with the League Championship trophy in 1988

We're going to audition for parts in a porny movie now that we've won the League in 1988". Billy McNeill is slightly more modestly dressed however.

"We're really the best of mates, aren't we, Terry?" "Of course, Roy!"

Henrik Larsson shoots for goal in the game against St Johnstone which won the League in May 1998.

Tom Boyd is now a dignified Ambassador for the club. He is far from dignified here, however.

Chris Sutton against Dundee United.

A League title, a car and a bottle of bubbly. What more could a man desire?

Henrik Larsson and Lubo Moravcik 2002.

Neil Lennon in unusual headgear.

Paul Hartley.

Georgios Samaras looking like a wasp in the yellow and black away strip against Hibs at Easter Road.

Leigh Griffiths shares a moment with Neil Lennon in a game against Hearts at Tynecastle.

"I'm telling you, it's going to be 10 in a row!"

Scott Brown congratulates goalkeeper Scott Bain after a good save at Ibrox.

Celebrations outside Celtic Park 2018.

Shocking pink! It was a shocking display as well, as Celtic failed to clinch the League at Easter Road in April 2018.

Double Treble icons beside the Celtic Star.

The really important people - the fans!

ER
UE
PIONS
ALL
MOVED
HAIL

CHAPTER 24

A GREAT SEASON

1968/69

There are those who claim that the football played by Celtic in 1968/69, certainly in the second part of the season, was the best they have ever played, better even than the great year of 1967. There were definitely some great games played by the team, which was still more or less the team which had won in Lisbon, although Jim Brogan had now replaced John Clark at left half and Bertie Auld was used more sparingly with John Hughes, who had missed out at Lisbon being deployed more often. George Connelly also made a few appearances this year. In addition, two players were bought in the course of the season – Tommy Callaghan from Dunfermline and Harry Hood from Clyde.

Like all good seasons, there were a few "wobbles". One was in September when a defeat by Rangers led to an "infectious" period when the team did not immediately bounce back, another was in December on frozen pitches and yet another when the end was in sight. But who can forget the wonderful calendar month of April when all three Scottish domestic trophies were secured – and that was in the wake of a heartbreaking exit from Europe at the hands of AC Milan?

And yet, both domestic League games against Rangers were lost. 1968/69 is an excellent example of how a defeat from Rangers need not be the end of the world, as some supporters seem to think it is. The important game is, as always, the next one and Jock Stein himself would always say categorically that the points you

Celtic 1968/69. Back Row: Brogan, O'Neill, Craig, Simpson, Fallon, Gemmell, Murdoch, Clark. Front Row: Johnstone, Lennox, Wallace, McNeill, Chalmers, Callaghan, Auld, Hughes.

gained from beating St Johnstone or Partick Thistle were just as valuable as those you gained from beating Rangers. Rangers' problem was just exactly that this season. They took four points from Celtic, but still finished five points behind!

The first such defeat from Rangers came as early as 14 September. To put it in some sort of perspective, Celtic had already beaten them twice in the Scottish League Cup, Bobby Murdoch was out injured and Bobby Lennox had a legitimate goal disallowed for offside. But Rangers won 4–2, and the press, as always, showed their true colours in hailing this great victory for Rangers with the *Glasgow Herald's* infamous headline "Rangers victory gives Scottish football new life" requiring no further comment.

Celtic then wobbled with a defeat to St Etienne in the European Cup and a draw at Dunfermline but the European situation was retrieved and Celtic got back on track with a few admittedly uneasy victories. These included the game against Dundee United (a 2–0 win) when Jimmy Johnstone showed public displeasure at being substituted and ended up being suspended for seven days. And that was after he had hid in the toilet fearing the wrath of big Jock and only emerging after Jock had promised not to hit him!

Often in this era, Celtic played their best football against Hibs, and never more so than in the game at Easter Road on 30 November, when they were 1–2 down with only 11 minutes left. They looked out of it until it was as if Jock Stein had suddenly pressed a switch, and Celtic won 5–2, simply devastating the Hibs defence with a couple of goals from Bobby Lennox, one from John Hughes and another from Billy McNeill.

A further five goals came against St Mirren the following Saturday before we hit trouble on the hard pitches and frost before the New Year with three successive draws against Falkirk, Kilmarnock and Airdrie causing concern. In spite of all that, Celtic finished 1968 still two points ahead of nearest challengers Dundee United with Rangers, in spite of having a Stein of their own (Colin whom they had bought from Hibs), in all sorts of travails.

New Year opened with a slight thaw, a 5–0 win over Clyde at Parkhead and a knighthood for Celtic's chairman Bob Kelly in the New Year's Honours List. Celtic supporters were ambivalent about the last of these three, for not everyone felt that it was deserved given Mr Kelly's role in the bad old days. The following day, 2 January, saw Celtic go to Ibrox and lose unluckily 0–1 after a penalty was given when a shot from Willie Henderson hit Billy McNeill on the arm. Hugh Taylor in the *Daily Record* disagreed with that decision, as indeed did most of the press, but Rangers took advantage and won 1–0.

Celtic's League campaign now teetered on the brink. Would there be another collapse caused by the "infection" of the Ibrox defeat? Fortunately not, and Celtic won their next three difficult games 3–1 against Dunfermline at Parkhead, Aberdeen at Pittodrie and Dundee United on a very rainy day at Tannadice. John Hughes, as often in bad weather conditions excelled but the game is also remembered for Pat McMahon's goal in one of his few appearances for the club.

There followed a very satisfying 5–0 defeat of Hearts, and the rest of February tended to be taken up with other competitions. Curiously, both 1 March and 1 April saw 3–2 wins over St Johnstone. The 1 March game was in the Scottish Cup, but the game at Muirton Park on 1 April was one of the many games that typified Celtic in those days. Down 0–2 and John Hughes off the field with a bad injury, Celtic nevertheless fought back to win 3–2 with Harry Hood scoring the winner in the last minute when the ball rebounded off a post.

That had followed a successful March (as far as the League campaign was concerned) which had seen wins over Arbroath, Raith Rovers, Partick Thistle, St Johnstone and a slightly disappointing 1–1 draw with Hibs. And thus began the month of April in which all three Scottish trophies were landed. (The League Cup final should have been played in October but was delayed by a fire at Hampden a few days before the scheduled event.) The 6–2 League Cup Final victory over Hibs was one of Celtic's best ever performances, and sugar was added with the news that Rangers had lost to Dundee United. Still flush with this success, Celtic then beat a stubborn and relegation threatened Falkirk 5–2 at Parkhead on the Wednesday night to put themselves within touching distance of the flag.

There followed a controversial game with Airdrie at Parkhead on 19 April when Celtic, having fought back to draw 2–2, then seemed to have the game won with a Billy McNeill goal which was given by the referee but disallowed by a brave Jungle side linesman. Billy rather lost the place with the linesman and was lucky not to be disciplined, but he did seem to have a point.

In the end it did not really matter all that much because Celtic went to Kilmarnock, needing to win to clinch the title. In the event, it was a 2–2 draw. Celtic once again showed their ability to come from behind. They were 0–2 down at half-time on a windy night, but gained a draw through an own goal and then a terrific drive from Tommy Gemmell late in the game. The players and fans treated this draw as if it were a win and had brought Celtic the League Championship.

Scottish Cup Final		
Celtic 4 Rangers 0	Hampden	26 April
Scottish League Cup Final		
Celtic 6 Hibs 2	Hampden	5 April
English Cup Final		
Manchester City 1 Leicester City 0	Wembley	25 April
English League Cup Final		
Swindon Town 3 Arsenal 1 a.e.t	Wembley	15 March
English League		
Leeds United		

Theoretically this wasn't quite true, for some outrageous scores might yet have thwarted Celtic, but in any case when Rangers lost at Dens Park the following night, the League was confirmed.

It had been another hard fought and rewarding Championship, the fourth in a row and the 24th overall, and Celtic went on to win the Scottish Cup on the Saturday after that by beating Rangers 4–0. There was, however, one spectacular piece of anticlimax on the following Monday when all three Scottish trophies were proudly paraded at Celtic Park before the game against Morton. This was very impressive – but then Morton scored three times in the first 10 minutes and eventually won the game 4–2!

CHAPTER 25

TAKING IT IN OUR STRIDE

1969/70

Season 1969/70 was one of Celtic's easiest League wins of the Jock Stein era. There were major disappointments in other tournaments at the end of the season, but the Scottish League was won with a degree of ease. Basically, Celtic kept winning, after a couple of hiccups early on, Rangers changed manager and suffered a major collapse, and Aberdeen and Hibs, who would put up more of a challenge in the early 1970s, had not yet risen.

Celtic's form this season could be absolutely devastating. As is often the case, games in December have a vital bearing on the destination of the Championship, and Celtic's December was brilliant – 4–1 over the strong St Johnstone at Muirton Park, 7–2 over Dundee United one rainy midweek night at Celtic Park, and the decade of the 1960s finishing with an 8–1 tanking of poor Partick Thistle.

The League season had not started quite so well with a 0–0 draw with St Johnstone on the first day of the League season at the end of August (Celtic had already qualified for the League Cup later stages), a defeat to Dunfermline at East End Park and then a puzzling reverse to Hibs at Celtic Park (which can only be put down to the "we played badly" and "they played well" explanation). These were in the first two weeks of September, but then Celtic registered a vital 1–0 win over Rangers in the Ibrox rain thanks to a goal from Harry Hood which he scored by turning Ron McKinnon and scoring sublimely. This was the time of the "Hare Krishna" movement in Great Britain, and their song was easily adapted to finish with "Harry Hood". It also probably strangled at birth any Rangers challenge for the League, for they were already suffering from a major Celtic complex, as Celtic had put them out of the League Cup. It was a grim time for the Ibrox men.

Summer 1969 had been poor for Rangers, as the 4–0 hammering in the Scottish Cup Final haunted them. The autumn was worse. In sheer desperation they brought back Jim Baxter from England. It was hailed as a great coup, and he was going to put Celtic in their place, the sycophants in the press told us. It was an embarrassment. Already suffering from problems with alcohol, "slim Jim" was fat, manifestly unfit and did not last until Christmas. But neither did manager Davie White.

The Celtic team was changing. In particular, the arrival of David Hay, a very versatile character who could play at right-back or right-half, was well appreciated. But Bobby Murdoch was struggling with weight problems, and men like Steve Chalmers and Bertie Auld were not used in the

A young and grim-looking Davie Hay.

forward line as often as they had been in the past. Harry Hood had now arrived, and John Hughes was playing better than ever, while in the goal John Fallon seemed to have taken over permanently from Ronnie Simpson. Tommy Gemmell was spectacularly dropped after an indiscretion while playing for Scotland, and, although things were patched up, the relationship between big Tam and big Jock were never quite the same again.

But the League Cup was won at the end of October and progress was made in Europe. Celtic, in spite of their few earlier blips, finished 1969 comfortably on top of the League. There had been one reverse in November as Celtic made it an Edinburgh double by losing to Hearts at Parkhead, a reverse partly to be explained by the imminence of a European tie against Benfica. It was also one of the first games that Kenny Dalglish played for the club. However, apart from the reverse to Hearts, things were more than satisfactory in the Scottish League as 1970 arrived, the thrashing of Partick Thistle meaning that Celtic were two points ahead of Rangers.

The New Year fixture against Rangers at a frosty Parkhead on 3 January was one of the less interesting encounters between these two but the goalless draw did at least retain Celtic's points advantage at the top, but from then on, Celtic's League form was more or less impeccable, the next League points being dropped on 25 March, when the League was virtually within Celtic's grasp.

The game at Easter Road on 17 January, for example, was a magnificent Celtic performance, typical of the way that they played against Hibs in those days. A crowd of over 40,000 were there in bitter January weather. There was a glorious McNeill header in the first half, and then after Hibs had equalised and looked to be heading for a not undeserved draw, in the closing minutes John Hughes broke through and scored with what seemed to be a miskick. Then Dunfermline were beaten in the Cup and the League in successive weeks, and then significantly in mid-February, Celtic beat Rangers in the Scottish Cup at Parkhead in a nasty game. It did not materially affect the Scottish League, of course, but it had a grave psychological effect, as once again Rangers failed to cope with Celtic's success with Celtic's high-profile European campaign of 1970 further depressing Rangers.

Five wins followed over Raith Rovers, Airdrie, Dundee United, Morton and Ayr United – a feature of all these games being the quality of goals scored by defenders Gemmell and McNeill in addition to those scored by the more recognised strikers. These games were important, but as they were played in the shadow of the European Cup campaign in which Celtic had reached the semi-final by the time that they beat Ayr United 3–0, it came almost as a surprise to realise that when Aberdeen came to Celtic Park on 25 March, a draw would win the League for the fifth year in a row. Such had been the collapse of Rangers and other challengers.

The game against Aberdeen was a major disappointment for the 33,000 fans who saw Celtic miss chances in the first half, lose two quick-fire goals in the second half and only pull one back through Tommy Gemmell at the end. The cynics all thought that it was a device to delay the winning of the League and to add spice to the Scottish Cup Final when the two teams would meet on 11 April, but this did less than justice to a hard-working Aberdeen side whom Eddie Turnbull was now fashioning into a force to be reckoned with. It was also, perhaps, the first sign of the complacency which would bring disastrous consequences upon Celtic later in the spring.

The League was won at Tynecastle on Saturday, 28 March. It was a game which did the Hearts persecution complex no harm at all as Jim Townsend was sent off for a fairly innocuous squaring up to Davie Hay, and then a penalty was awarded for an offence that seemed to be outside the box. Not that it mattered, for Tommy Gemmell missed it! No goals were scored at all, although there were a few near things at each end, but the 0–0 draw, allied to Rangers' feckless 1–1 draw at home to Airdrie, meant that Celtic were now seven points clear with only three games left and could not be caught.

It was a comprehensive lifting of the Championship for the 25th time, but it has been overshadowed by what happened next. The League being in the bag as well as the League Cup at an early stage meant that Celtic could now deal with their (and the media's) obsession with Leeds United. They duly did so comprehensively, but not without side effects. Celtic have tended to hide behind poor refereeing when talking about the Scottish Cup Final against Aberdeen. The refereeing was indeed poor, with three dreadful decisions given against Celtic at key points, but it was not the only factor – the two others being that Aberdeen played well and Celtic failed to raise their game when they needed to. Perhaps the ease with which they won the League had something to do with that?

The European Cup Final is another long and painful story...

Scottish Cup Final		
Aberdeen 3 Celtic 1	Hampden	11 April
Scottish League Cup Final		
Celtic 1 St Johnstone 0	Hampden	25 October
European Cup Final		
Feyenoord 2 Celtic 1 aet	Milan	6 May
English Cup Final		
Chelsea 2 Leeds United 1	Old Trafford	29 April
(after 2-2 draw aet at Wembley on 11 April)		
English League Cup Final		
Manchester City 2 WBA 1	Wembley	7 March
English League		
Everton		

CHAPTER 26

"TELL ME THE OLD, OLD STORY"

1970/71

In normal circumstances, losing a European Cup Final is not considered to be a monumental disaster. After all, it means that you are the second-best team in Europe – hardly suicidal stuff – and in Celtic's case in 1970, they were indisputably the best in Great Britain after their fine win over Leeds United in April in the semi-final. Yet summer 1970 was a dreadful time, because Celtic had been the favourites to beat Feyenoord and win the European Cup again. An ill-advised tour of America took place not long after the European Cup Final defeat, money rose too high on the agenda, some players behaved like spoilt brats, everybody got homesick and even the manager took the huff and went home early! Oh dear, we prefer not to think of that awful summer!

What was clear was that a different team would have to be evolved. "Evolved" was the key word. No sudden dramatic sackings or expensive foreign imports, but rather the gradual development of youngsters like McGrain, Connelly, Macari and Dalglish (Hay had already established himself) while all the time the experienced members of the squad would keep their place, at least for a spell. Stein did all this, and his winning of the League in such circumstances was one of his best achievements. He had had a major disappointment in Milan and deserved his share of the blame, but after taking it on the chin, Jock fought back and won his sixth Championship in a row.

The season was characterised by the black events at New Year, now called the Ibrox Disaster, when 66 Rangers supporters lost their lives. It happened at the end of the Rangers v. Celtic game, and remains one of Scottish football's saddest days. In footballing terms, Rangers who had been off to a reasonable start, even beating Celtic narrowly in the League Cup final, could not really cope with the consequences and their League season, at least, imploded, as they finished fourth behind Celtic, Aberdeen and St Johnstone.

St Johnstone had a good season, but Celtic's real challengers were Aberdeen. The Dons had, of course, won the Scottish Cup last season in a controversial final against Celtic and this year they impressed from an early stage. Eddie Turnbull, always a dour competitor and an old rival of Jock Stein from their playing days in the 1950s, had built up a good side with Joe Harper and ex-Rangers players Jim Forrest and Alex Willoughby showing their ability to score goals, and they also became very proficient at their offside trap. Offside traps don't always work and are dependent on defenders having

Celtic walk out to play Clyde on 1 May 1971 at a Celtic Park in the throes of having the Main Stand renovated.

the speed to get forward at the right time. They are equally dependent on an efficient linesman who can spot such things. But this Aberdeen defence, who had had their fingers burnt more than once in the past by the speed of Bobby Lennox, had worked on it and it had served them well.

Celtic's League season started well and featured a good 2–0 over Rangers at Parkhead which was far more comprehensive than it appeared. John Hughes and Bobby Murdoch scored the goals that day. Thereafter, apart from a reverse in mid-September to Hibs at Easter Road in which ex-Celt Joe McBride scored twice for Hibs, Celtic remained comparatively accident-free (apart from a dismal goalless draw to Falkirk at Brockville in November) until Aberdeen came to Celtic Park on the foggy, frosty day of 12 December.

An excellent crowd of 63,000 turned up for this game, showing the world that a successful Aberdeen side could draw the crowds, and they saw a narrow but decisive 1–0 win for Aberdeen, the goal coming from an opportunist Joe Harper header. Thereafter, hard as Celtic tried, they could not break down the Dons defence, falling foul of the offside trap once or twice, and the full-time whistle meant that Aberdeen were now one point ahead of Celtic.

The Dons maintained and enhanced their lead over the New Year winning over Dundee, St Johnstone and Kilmarnock (while the Ibrox Disaster game ended in a draw for Celtic), but 16 January was a significant day for Celtic. Not only did Celtic turn on their best performance of the season by beating Dundee 8–1 at Dens Park with the veteran Bertie Auld totally outstanding, but Hibs, who had beaten Celtic earlier in the season, did the same against Aberdeen, winning 2–1. On 6 February both Celtic and Aberdeen lost, Aberdeen to Dunfermline and Celtic to St Johnstone. Jock Stein was angry with John Hughes, whom he took off – the beginning of the end of any kind of relationship that may have existed between the two of them – and also with his defence who conceded three goals from high balls into the box, something that seemed to point the finger at Billy McNeill. However, the news from Dunfermline took the edge off things.

More help came Celtic's way on 20 February from an unlikely source when Rangers held Aberdeen to a goalless draw at Pittodrie, while Celtic beat Airdrie 4–1. This meant that Celtic, if they won their game in hand, would be on top of Aberdeen. Both teams then dropped a further point, Aberdeen to Motherwell on 3 April, and Celtic to Dundee United on 10 April. By this time, because of Celtic's other commitments, they were actually three games and five points behind the Dons. It was now clear that the game at Pittodrie between the two clubs on 17 April would be very significant, especially after Celtic beat Motherwell 3–0 on Monday, 12 April.

At this stage there was more than a little speculation about the future of Jock Stein. Newspapers continued to carry stories that he was going to Old Trafford next year to take over Manchester United. Jock had no such intentions, for by his own admission he got homesick about 10 miles south of Glasgow, but he was enjoying watching the press make a fool of themselves saying things like "talks had taken place" and "he was close to accepting the post". ("Sources close to the club" had told them that – and that usually means that they had made it up themselves!) At this point in the team's hotel at Stonehaven the day before the game Stein told his players that he would be at Celtic Park next year, and the players all got a boost because of that, not least because the press had made a fool of themselves!

The game at Pittodrie was a 1–1 draw, something which suited Celtic down to the ground. On a dry and bumpy pitch after some overnight snow, Harry Hood scored early for Celtic, and although Alex Willoughby equalised for Aberdeen, Celtic held out and drew 1–1 with Billy McNeill and goalkeeper Evan Williams outstanding.

Celtic now had three games left, and Aberdeen one, with a three-point differential. The following week, Celtic who were now playing at Hampden so that Celtic Park's stand could be renovated were idle because their game against Ayr United was rained off, but in the meantime, Aberdeen, aware now that Celtic held the initiative, blew up at Falkirk, losing 0–1. Their League programme was now finished, and Celtic had only to take three points from their remaining three games to win the League on goal average, and four to be absolutely sure.

Three games had to be played in a week. A 2–2 draw with St Mirren at Love Street on the Tuesday night was followed by a 2–0 win over Ayr on the Thursday at Hampden. These goals were scored by Lennox and Wallace and effectively gave Celtic the League before a piece of theatre on the Saturday, 1 May when the Lisbon Lions took the field for one last time before some of them were due to depart for other clubs. Still more theatrical was the return to Celtic Park, even though it resembled a building site, which indeed it was.

To lose the League, Celtic would have had to lose by some impossible score, but they won 6–1, with the prolific Bobby Lennox scoring a hat-trick. 35,000 people departed happy, having seen their team win the League for six years in a row and equalling the feat of the magnificent men who performed between 1904 and 1910. How nice it was also to have in the squad one Jimmy Quinn, grandson of the great Jimmy of long ago. It was the "old, old story" and Celtic fans once again walked tall.

Scottish Cup Final		
Celtic 2 Rangers 1	Hampden	12 May
(after 1-1 draw at Hampden on 8 May)		
Scottish League Cup Final		
Rangers 1 Celtic 0	Hampden	24 October
English Cup Final		
Arsenal 2 Liverpool 1 aet	Wembley	8 May
English League Cup Final		
Tottenham Hotspur 2 Aston Villa 0	Wembley	27 February
English League		
Arsenal		

CHAPTER 27

WITH A DEGREE OF EASE

1971/72

Season 1971/72 was another remarkable season in the history of Celtic FC. There were spectacular moments in all the other three competitions, good and bad, but the Scottish League was, in the main, a solid and steady progression to the Championship, which of course, being the seventh in a row, beat the record set by Maley's Edwardians, now well over 60 years ago.

Celtic lost only two League games – one to St Johnstone (a hard team who often gave Celtic a great deal of trouble in those days) and one to Hearts when the season was virtually all over. Two great players emerged this season. One was Kenny Dalglish who had been knocking on the door for some time and now came good, and the other was John "Dixie" Deans signed in what seemed to be either a fit of pique or a panic attack on the part of Jock Stein. The pair of them were outstanding successes.

Rangers had a curious season. Celtic had beaten them three times (all at Ibrox) by the middle of September, and they then more or less disappeared out of the League race, finishing 16 points behind Celtic in third place. They were defeated by Hibs in the semi-final of the Scottish Cup... and then won the European Cup-winners' Cup – something that said a great deal about the strength of Scottish football at that time! Cynics however pointed out that their European success came in the only tournament where they did not have to face Celtic!

Celtic's European foray ended heartbreakingly in a penalty shoot-out defeat to Inter Milan at the semi-final stage. This was a shame because it was felt that Celtic could do well in the Final, but neither they nor Inter Milan could break each other's defensive iron curtain. Fortunately for Dixie Deans, the only man to miss a penalty, he bounced back and scored a hat-trick in the Scottish Cup Final.

Deans had joined Celtic in the wake of the previous Cup Final, the League Cup Final in October. Without Billy McNeill, Celtic went into the game against little-fancied Partick Thistle and managed to lose 4–1. Stein's reaction was to buy Dixie Deans from Motherwell, whom one suspects that Motherwell were quite keen to lose and get money for. Deans was currently serving a suspension and had a reputation for troublemaking. It turned out to be one of Stein's best ever moves.

The League campaign opened in astonishing fashion with a 9–1 defeat of Clyde at Celtic Park. It will be recalled that in the last League meeting of the last season, Celtic beat the same opposition 6–1 at Celtic Park. Here the slaughter of the East End neighbours continued with Bobby Lennox scoring a hat-trick

Kenny Dalglish.

with his phenomenal speed, and the very impressive young Lou Macari adding a couple. Then came a 3–2 win at Ibrox. Rangers had a fair amount of the play that day, but, having been beaten by Celtic 3–0 and 2–0 in the League Cup, were psyched out once again by the green and white jerseys. Two wins over Morton and Airdrie followed, the win over Morton being particularly satisfying as the Greenock men had defeated Celtic in the League Cup sectional stage.

Then came the visit of St Johnstone. St Johnstone usually played well against Celtic and today they won 1–0, a feature of the game being the many easy chances that Celtic missed with Macari and Wallace particularly profligate, and Jimmy Johnstone earning the wrath of the crowd by his insistence on beating a man twice when once would have done. Such a poor forward display had rarely been seen at Celtic Park since the pre-Stein days, and it might have been this game which started Stein thinking about Dixie Deans. The League Cup Final (another awful display by the forwards) may have forced him into action, but it was possibly this game against the men from Perth which planted the seed.

Stein's ire was a terrible thing, and there was a lot less feckless forward play in future. The following week saw Celtic win 1–0 at Hibs with a goal from Lou Macari, and there was further evidence of the development of the young "Quality Street" kids the next week when Kenny Dalglish scored a hat-trick to beat Dundee. Hughes and Wallace, having fallen badly out of favour with Jock Stein were dispatched to Crystal Palace, and several others of the old guard, even Murdoch, Johnstone and McNeill were told that they would have to up their game.

One of their best games of the season came at Tannadice Park on 13 November, a week after a hard-fought draw against Aberdeen, the closest challengers. The Aberdeen game had been characterised by a bizarre own goal from Billy McNeill, after which some Celtic supporters began to ask questions about his future. But at Tannadice, a lacklustre Celtic were 0–1 down at half-time to Dundee United, a team who always played well at home. It was depressing but once again "a button was pressed". Jimmy Johnstone was given a roving commission and was seen on the left as often as on the right, Kenny Dalglish moved forward, and by the 80th minute Celtic were 5–1 up, scoring more or less at will, and the Tannadice home support evaporated as Harry Hood scored twice (one from a penalty) and Lennox, Macari and Dalglish scored the others. No one questioned Billy McNeill's future after this game!

The last six games of the year saw six emphatic wins including three 5–1 victories and the year of 1971 was concluded on Christmas Day with a 3–2 win over Hearts at Celtic Park, the last time that Celtic played a game on Christmas Day itself, the dropping of the Christmas Day fixture being an indication that Christmas was now slowly becoming as important as New Year in Scotland.

All this meant that Celtic entered 1972 one point ahead of Aberdeen who were similarly enjoying a good run of form. Following the hammering of Clyde, Celtic took on Rangers at Parkhead. With the teams locked at 1–1 and neither team having any great advantage, the unlikely source of Jim Brogan the left-back scored with a header, appearing out of nowhere to do so.

A point was dropped against Morton on 8 January, but apart from that, progress continued to be made. By this time, a very significant political thing happened when a miners' strike was called. It would be February before the effects were felt, and it did not have any great impact on the football season (as it would in 1974, for example) but it certainly did effect the population at large with power cuts and some frightening scenes on picket lines. The government gave in, but this issue would not go away. At the end of January, there was also the horrendous event in Northern Ireland, now known as Bloody Sunday.

Aberdeen had already dropped a few more points, but were still in the race when they presented Celtic the League Championship with an astonishing own goal. On Leap Year's Day, 29 February, they transferred centre-half and captain Martin Buchan to Manchester United! It was the equivalent of Winston Churchill selling the Spitfires in the middle of the Battle of Britain, and it can only be explained away in terms of sheer greed with little concern for the interests of their supporters. It got its own reward as the Dons title challenge now fizzled out and it would take several years before their supporters forgave them.

The folly of selling Buchan came apparent when Celtic came to Aberdeen on 11 March and both teams played out a tight 1–1 draw. Aberdeen had to win to have any sort of chance, but the draw meant that even Jock Stein himself, usually reluctant to make any premature statements, said that it was Celtic's title.

Celtic were now more concerned with other competitions, but they suffered a bad blow on 25 March when young Danny McGrain, a very impressive full-back, fractured his skull in a collision with a Falkirk player. Celtic still won 1–0, and the title was confirmed on 15 April with four games to spare when Celtic beat East Fife 3–0 before a packed crowd of 12,000 at Bayview, Methil, the atmosphere reminding the locals of their own great days of 20 years ago.

And so Celtic had beaten their own record of six-in-a-row between 1905 and 1910. They seemed capable of going on for some time yet as far as the League were concerned, such was their ability to paralyse opponents. There was also the perpetual producing of young talent as the great Celtic side kept reinventing itself, and doing so seamlessly.

Scottish Cup Final		
Celtic 6 Hibs 1	Hampden	6 May
Scottish League Cup Final		
Partick Thistle 4 Celtic 1	Hampden	23 October
English Cup Final		
Leeds United 1 Arsenal 0	Wembley	6 May
English League Cup Final		
Stoke City 2 Chelsea 1	Wembley	4 March
English League		
Derby County		

CHAPTER 28

A CLOSE RUN THING

1972/73

In all the "nine-in-a-row" years from 1965/66 to 1973/74, this one was the most difficult. In the other years, Celtic were clearly the best team in Scotland, sometimes as in 1970, 1972 and 1974, for example, overwhelmingly so. This was not necessarily the case all season in 1972/73 but it is to the credit of Jock Stein and his men that they won through at the end, in spite of a major crisis in the middle of the season. There was an uncharacteristically early exit from Europe, and the two domestic trophies were lost, perhaps unluckily, in the finals to Hibs and Rangers. The League was therefore the only trophy won this season.

One could argue that the best team in Scotland was Hibs. They certainly played the best football on occasion, but lacked the consistency to maintain the pace. Rangers had definitely improved since last year and took Celtic all the way to the last day of the season, but Aberdeen, although always a force to be reckoned with, had not yet recovered from their grievous self-inflicted blow of selling Martin Buchan last season, and the pall of depression continued to hang over the north-east.

Celtic's League season started well with wins over Kilmarnock and Morton, and then came a most unusual Old Firm encounter. The game had to be played at Hampden because of a fire in the stand at Celtic Park and it kicked off at 12.00 partly as an anti-hooliganism measure and partly because Queen's Park were playing Stranraer at 3.00 p.m.! In spite of the unconventional nature of all this, Rangers still approached this game like a man going to the dentist and duly lost 3–1. When John Greig scored a late consolation goal for Rangers, he was given a cheer by the Celtic fans because there were no Rangers supporters left!

But then Celtic went down 0–2 to Dundee at Dens Park. Dundee were to give Celtic a fair amount of bother this season, and on this day, one can say nothing other than that they deserved to win their first League win over Celtic at Dens Park since the days of Alan Gilzean and Ian Ure in November 1961. It would however be Celtic's only League defeat until the New Year, although a draw against Airdrie on 7 October at Parkhead would result in a certain amount of dissatisfaction among the crowd.

Celtic fans at Easter Road when the eighth Championship in a row was secured. One of the flags seems to be out of date!

Round about the turn of the year, Celtic were plunged into crisis with five on-the-surface unrelated events, but only a fool would have thought them entirely unconnected. Hibs beat Celtic in the Scottish League Cup Final on 9 December, a flu epidemic hit the players at Celtic Park causing a couple of postponements, Jock Stein was admitted to a Glasgow hospital with severe chest pains (looking for all the world like a heart attack) Rangers beat Celtic 2–1 in the New Year fixture on 6 January and then Lou Macari, who had looked unhappy for some time, asked for a transfer. Clearly all these events impacted on the others, and the Christmas and New Year period was a far from happy time at Celtic Park.

There were other problems as well. Murdoch was out, struggling once again with fitness problems, Johnstone could be infuriatingly inconsistent sometimes and Dalglish seemed to be suffering from what might be called "second season syndrome", a phenomenon whereby a youngster makes a great impact in his first season, but is less successful in his second season because he has now been "sussed" by opponents. There seemed to be a problem with goalkeeping with neither Evan Williams nor Denis Connaghan entirely fitting the bill, and Celtic moved for Ally Hunter of Kilmarnock. The supporters were unhappy about the loss of the Scottish League Cup Final (the third in a row that they had lost) and weren't always as encouraging as one would have liked. And the danger signals went up with a defeat by Airdrie at Broomfield at the end of January.

Yet Celtic came through it. The flu epidemic disappeared, Stein was back in harness by early February after coming out of hospital and having a few days' rest, and things began to tighten up. There were two unsatisfactory draws in February, one of them being an astonishing game at Methil when three separate Celtic players – Murdoch, Hood and Dalglish – all missed penalties, and it was only a glancing header from Dixie Deans in the last minute which earned Celtic a point. Another draw came at Tannadice in March when veteran Bobby Lennox scored the two goals. Rangers were going well also – although they too were fallible – and the season was heading to an exciting climax.

Celtic, however, seemed to have hit form just at the right moment of the season with all their key men back after injuries and fitness problems. Particularly beneficial was the experience of Bobby Murdoch. Jimmy Johnstone now hit top form as well as Dixie Deans began to emphasise, as if we did not know it already, what a great acquisition he had been. Celtic beat Falkirk, Hearts and Motherwell, and their victory at the difficult ground of Muirton Park, Perth on 14 April meant that the position at the top of the table left no margin for error. Celtic were two points behind but had a game in hand and a far better goal difference. Celtic had three games, Rangers two.

The game in hand was against Dumbarton at Parkhead and it was played off on Wednesday, 18 April. The 5–0 victory meant that Celtic were now top of the table and the goal difference was now so overwhelmingly in Celtic's favour that there was no way that Rangers could hope to beat Celtic by that method. Their only hope lay in Celtic losing one of their remaining two games – to Arbroath at home or (more likely) to Hibs at Easter Road – and themselves winning both of their games. They had Aberdeen at Pittodrie, and then East Fife at Ibrox.

What added spice to all this was that it was now known that the Scottish Cup Final this year would also be Celtic v. Rangers, both clubs having won their respective semi-finals. Thus the last three Saturdays of the season would decide both the Scottish League and the Scottish Cup. For a neutral, this was great and the climax to the Scottish season attracted a great deal of interest in England and elsewhere.

The game at Celtic Park on 21 April was played in lovely spring sunshine, conditions in which Celtic often revel and a great second-half performance saw Celtic beat lowly Arbroath 4–0 with second-half goals from Deans, Hood, Hay and an own goal scored by one-time Pittodrie favourite Ernie Winchester and now coming to the end of his career with the Gayfield men.

But Celtic Park was also listening to its collective "trannie", with even Jock Stein himself caught by a press photographer with a radio beside him so that he could listen to Aberdeen v. Rangers. He would normally have disapproved most strongly about all this, but such was the tension, laced with a little optimism, for his side were now playing with reassurance and skill.

The League indeed might have been won that day, but Rangers' late equaliser at Pittodrie meant that it all had to go to the last day. Celtic knew that a draw would be enough for them at Easter Road. Hibs had themselves dropped out of the race for the League, but were still having one of their better seasons and Celtic v. Hibs games at that time had a deserved reputation for great football.

"Shoals and shoals" of Celtic supporters (sadly not all of them well behaved) attended Easter Road that pleasant spring day. 45,453 saw a competent and

Dixie Deans has just scored against Hibs. He is pursued here by Kenny Dalglish.

Scottish Cup Final		
Rangers 3 Celtic 2	Hampden	5 May
Scottish League Cup Final		
Hibs 2 Celtic 1	Hampden	9 December
English Cup Final		
Sunderland 1 Leeds United 0	Wembley	5 May
English League Cup Final		
Spurs 1 Norwich City 0	Wembley	3 March
English League		
Liverpool		

professional performance with Celtic winning 3–0 (two goals from Deans and one from Dalglish) to land their eighth title in a row. Ian Archer of the *Glasgow Herald* described this season's League race as "uniquely exciting". "Nerve-wracking" is the way that most Celtic supporters would have described it, but the feeling of triumph was a glorious one, and one that, frankly, did not seem likely at the turn of the year.

CHAPTER 29

NINE IN A ROW

1973/74

It would probably be true to say that Celtic's ninth successive League Championship did not arouse as much excitement as the previous ones did. There were several reasons for this. One was that Celtic did get it rather easy, winning the League with three games to spare at Falkirk three days after a major European defeat and therefore in a strange atmosphere of anticlimax. The League was won by four points from Hibs but even that is deceptive, for Celtic lost points after the League was won when youngsters were given a run out and everyone was keeping themselves for the Scottish Cup Final.

But there were other reasons as well. The season was dominated by the fact that Scotland would be in the World Cup finals in Germany. Spice was added to this with the knowledge that England wouldn't – something that pleased the narrow-minded (about 98% of the population!) – and the International success did tend to take a little glitter away from the domestic season, even in the hearts and minds of those who normally professed to have little interest in the Scotland team (a breed that one finds rather too often among the Celtic support).

Slowly, there was a sea change in the attitude to the Scotland team. Gradually, and it would take time, Scotland ceased to be identified with Rangers. Rangers supporters used to go to Scotland games to boo Celtic players or any Anglo-Scot who happened to be a Roman Catholic, but that slowly altered and now in the 2010s we have gone full circle to discover that Rangers supporters, with their love of the Union Jack and the British Crown, are more likely to be anti-Scotland! In 1973/74 it was in fact Celtic who provided the backbone for the Scotland team with Davie Hay, Jimmy Johnstone, Kenny Dalglish and a few others.

While this was happening, the authorities now began to take seriously the problem of falling gates. Celtic's continued domination was certainly a factor, and this was the season when a new blueprint for League structure was brought out for discussion. So too was a belated realisation that facilities would have to improve. The idea that standing in heavy rain of a Saturday afternoon on uncovered terracings was what made Scotland great was now beginning to lose ground, as was the idea that it was acceptable for a ground to have zero toilet facilities for ladies and only basic unhygienic ones for men. That too was a slow process.

There were other factors as well, less immediately related to football. The Irish problem continued unabated, the miners had another overtime ban and

Jock Stein.

then a strike, this one leading to a three-day week and the allowing of football on a Sunday for the first time ever. Problems in the coalmining industry led to a General Election in February and then another one in October, and if we add in to that the resignation of the US President because of the cover-up of a burglary and general corruption, another war in the Middle East and the general acceptance that worldwide inflation was out of control, we can get some idea of how "busy" a year it was and how the Scottish League struggled to reach the headlines sometimes.

Hibs came second, but it was another dark year for Rangers who seemed to lose interest, especially when their stern Presbyterianism did not allow them to play on a Sunday. Aberdeen huffed and puffed for a while, but their time had passed (at least temporarily) and Celtic were able to lose four League games (including two shockers in a row to Motherwell and then Dundee in early February) and still win the League comfortably, as well as winning the Scottish Cup and reaching the semi-final of the European Cup before being (literally) "kicked off the park" by a bunch of thugs masquerading as Atletico Madrid.

Celtic had many fine players. Kenny Dalglish and Dixie Deans were consistently among the goals, and in midfield Davie Hay (after settling a rather absurd "contract dispute" which looked to the supporters more like a personality clash between the player and Jock Stein) was top rate playing alongside Steve Murray who had now taken over the role of Bobby Murdoch. Of the Lisbon Lions only Billy McNeill, Bobby Lennox and Jimmy Johnstone were still active with the club.

Only one defeat was sustained in the Scottish League before the New Year, and that was at Muirton Park, Perth – a traditional bogey ground for Celtic. In this case, the strong wind and the fact that five Celtic players had been with the triumphant Scotland squad in midweek were used as excuses, but there was something generally about that wide pitch and the quaint, almost rural atmosphere of the ground within touching distance of an ice rink and a whisky distillery that Celtic did not always cope with.

Perth was however only a momentary lapse. Deans scored six as Celtic beat Partick 7–0 in November (Jimmy McGrory's record of eight was never in more danger than on that day!) and then on the Saturdays both sides of Christmas came two 6–0 thrashings of poor Falkirk and Dunfermline Athletic from an angry Celtic team, angry because they had been compelled to play the League Cup Final on 15 December on a totally unsuitable pitch on an awful day and had lost 1–0 to Tommy Gemmell's Dundee.

The victory over Rangers on 5 January was a great deal easier than the 1–0 scoreline would have suggested, and that result more or less finished Rangers for the season. The two defeats at the beginning of February may well have opened the door ever so slightly for a League challenge from Hibs, but it was firmly closed again on 23 February when Celtic beat them 4–2 at Easter Road in a thriller which was 2–2 at one point in the second half before Paul Wilson, a grossly underrated player, scored the third and then Kenny Dalglish sealed it at the end. Hibs once again, a great team with great players, lacked a wee bit of "bottle" at the end.

Celtic were now back in the driving seat, and although there was a defeat to Partick Thistle (significantly perhaps in the wake of a stiff European test against Basle), three important victories over Dundee United, East Fife and Aberdeen between the first and second legs of the European Cup semi-final against Atletico Madrid meant that a draw against Falkirk at Brockville on 27 April would win the League for Celtic.

In some ways it was an anticlimax. Celtic had exited Europe to Atletico Madrid in midweek (death threats had been sent to Jimmy Johnstone by some Spanish supporters), and they were a tired team in a game which, apart from one moment of magic, seldom rose above the mediocre. The one good moment was a brilliant individual goal from Kenny Dalglish, and that was enough to earn the point to give Celtic their ninth successive League Championship. Yet even that was slightly upstaged by the news that day from England that Manchester United had been relegated!

Nevertheless, as the players ran round Brockville celebrating their ninth in a row, even those who were anti-Celtic in the media had to confess that this was some achievement, and nothing but the greatest credit had to be given to the man who had done it all – Jock Stein, the man who had revolutionised football in this country. He was possibly the most famous Scotsman of them all in England, second only to Robert Burns, and he was instantly recognised in England and much respected there.

As far as Celtic were concerned, if Willie Maley was the man who made Celtic, Stein was the man who rescued Celtic. If one could have gone back a decade to the awful days of April 1964 where the team could play good football occasionally but couldn't win anything, and tell a supporter that by 1974 Celtic would win nine in a row, one would have been considered a strong candidate for a visit to a mental hospital.

Celtic now went on to win the Scottish Cup as well, beating Dundee United in a rather one-sided Cup Final, and then Scotland went to Germany to perform reasonably well in the World Cup, and to return without disgrace.

Scottish Cup Final		
Celtic 3 Dundee United 0	Hampden	4 May
Scottish League Cup Final		
Dundee 1 Celtic 0	Hampden	15 December
English Cup Final		
Liverpool 3 Newcastle United 0	Wembley	4 May
English League Cup Final		
Wolves 2 Manchester City 1	Wembley	2 March
English League		
Leeds United		

CHAPTER 30

JOCK'S LAST TRIUMPH

1976/77

Jock Stein suffered serious injuries in a car crash in summer 1975. This meant that he was out of action for all the 1975/76 season. "When the cat's away, the mice will play…" and Rangers won a treble that year. With all due respect to that excellent lieutenant Sean Fallon, he was no Jock Stein. But Jock returned for the 1976/77 season. In some ways, it was his best ever. The standard of play was not great with very few players able to stand any sort of comparison with the great men of 10 years ago, but Stein made a few shrewd signings and repeatedly won the propaganda battle over Rangers in the media with one particularly spectacular coup in the spring.

Since the last time that the League title had been won in 1974, the League structure itself had changed. The Premier League now contained only 10 teams, and everyone played each other four times. Whether this was a good thing or not can be argued, but it certainly did mean that more games were meaningful, and that relegation was a live issue for many teams. 1976/77 opened, for example, with the Premier League bereft of Dundee and Celtic's particular bogey team, St Johnstone.

The start of the season was distinctly unimpressive. One particular game at Tannadice Park (a 0–1 defeat) saw a section of the support turn on Kenny Dalglish, and then a draw with Hearts at Celtic Park did not fire anyone with enthusiasm either, but gradually the team began to come together. There were two surprise signings. One was a little-known forward called Joe Craig from Partick Thistle, and the other turned a few heads when Stein signed Pat Stanton from Hibs. Pat had had an illustrious (although somewhat unproductive in terms of medals) career with Hibs and Scotland, but now, at nearly 33, looked past his best. Jock begged to differ, and it was a great signing. The Hibs stalwart became a Celtic hero.

There was also captain Kenny Dalglish, capable of winning any game, and a rapidly developing Roy Aitken. The defensive setup of Peter Latchford, Danny McGrain and Andy Lynch was more than adequate, and up front there was the ever willing Johnny Doyle, and a talented ball player called Ronnie Glavin. It was an adequate squad, although far from a world-beating one, as was proved by an early European exit to Wisla Krakow.

Domestically, things improved, but there seemed to be a problem with Aberdeen. Aberdeen were now managed by Ally MacLeod, a bouncy character who had the capability of knocking the dour Jock Stein off the headlines. He also managed to beat Celtic twice – once at Pittodrie and the

Alfie Conn rocks Scottish football and confounds a few bigots by signing for Celtic.

other (painfully) in the League Cup Final in a game where the phrase "bad luck" did not quite cover it. It hurt, but a more sober analysis reflected that the Cup-tied Stanton and Craig had not been eligible for this game, and that there was still a long time of the season to go.

Celtic now picked up, a key victory being the game at Tynecastle on 20 November 1976 when the team came back from twice being two goals behind to win 4–3 with Ronnie Glavin and Roy Aitken outstanding. This game was pivotal to both clubs. Celtic never looked back whereas Hearts never recovered and were duly relegated at the end of the season.

Celtic then beat Rangers at Ibrox on the following Wednesday night in spite of Bobby Lennox being carried off with a broken leg. (To his credit, John Greig was upset about his part in this, and duly went to hospital to visit Bobby.) Joe Craig scored a wonderful goal that night, and when Celtic also beat Rangers at Parkhead on 11 January, Rangers' title challenge looked dead in the water. On another front, as well, Rangers were struggling. Their fans had rioted in a friendly match in England, and in the wake of this, Willie Waddell (and how it must have hurt!) announced that from now on, Roman Catholic players would be welcome at Ibrox. They did not in fact sign anyone of that persuasion for many years, but the fans stayed away in any case. Jokes went around that Rangers did in fact play a Catholic – but he beat them 2–1!

It was now that Stein showed all his understanding of the situation by pouncing like a boxer on an opponent with a cut eye. Alfie Conn, ex-Rangers but now with Tottenham Hotspur, wanted home and became available. Stein went for him, having made great play about the fact that he had consulted his two senior players Danny McGrain and Kenny Dalglish. Shrewd observers picked up that Stein, McGrain and Dalglish, great Celts all, had something in common concerning religion! Conn was duly signed, and the "moral high ground" was not so much captured as was developed and had houses built on it! Conn was immediately welcomed by the Celtic support, as the impotent Rangers, trapped in their own cocoon of historical bigotry, looked on in vain.

Aberdeen were still a threat, however. They drew with Celtic on Boxing Day at Parkhead, and then won at Pittodrie on 5 March on the day that Alfie Conn made his first appearance as a substitute. But Celtic were still ahead and in any case, Aberdeen were hit by rumours of a match-fixing scandal. There was probably nothing in it, but it did have an effect on the team which had gone out of the Scottish Cup and now subsided in the Scottish League while the effervescent Ally MacLeod, temporarily quietened, departed the scene, heading for his Argentina nemesis in 1978.

Celtic duly won the League, but 19 March at Ibrox saw a fan flare up when goalkeeper Peter Latchford was injured in trying to prevent Rangers going 2–1 up. From the Celtic end, it looked like a foul, and cans and bottles were thrown. Jock Stein immediately went round and calmed the storm, and a few Celtic players were also seen to defuse the situation. Potential riot then descended into farcical humour when Roy Aitken scored an immediate equaliser, and we had the sight of Rangers fans, scarves in the air singing the praises of their team until Roy scored. The scarves all come down suddenly and morose, angry silence descended on that part of the ground. Alfie Conn, booed and jeered all game by the Rangers fans, answered by playing brilliantly.

The injury to Latchford was quite serious, but fortunately Celtic had an adequate replacement in the much-travelled Roy Baines, and he provided another moment of humour by psyching out Dundee United's goalkeeper Hamish McAlpine, as McAlpine took a penalty and missed at Celtic Park on 26 March! Then on the night that Celtic might have won the League at Motherwell on 13 April, Andy Lynch managed to score two own goals to prevent it happening! Had he scored again, it would have been a hat-trick!

The League was eventually won on 16 April at Easter Road. A Joe Craig goal was enough to do it, but there was a rather bitter taste left in the mouth by Hibs' refusal to allow BBC or STV to show highlights of the game. It was difficult to read anything into this other than sheer spite and jealousy and the thought of Pat Stanton winning his only League medal in front of his Hibs fans – but for another club! But then again jealousy of Celtic has been a sad and recurrent theme of the Easter Road boardroom since the 1890s!

So Jock had come back and done it again. It was a memorable season, and icing was added to the cake when Celtic won the Scottish Cup as well, beating Rangers 1–0 in what was generally regarded to be one of the worst Scottish Cup Finals of them all. The rain was incessant, and most people watched it on TV. But it was another double for Celtic. It would, however, be Stein's last, for trouble was fast developing.

Scottish Cup Final		
Celtic 1 Rangers 0	Hampden	7 May
Scottish League Cup Final		
Aberdeen 2 Celtic 1 aet	Hampden	6 November
English Cup Final		
Manchester United 2 Liverpool 1	Wembley	21 May
English League Cup Final		
Aston Villa 3 Everton 2 aet	Old Trafford	13 April
(after 2-2 at Wembley, and 1-1 aet at Hillsborough)		
English League		
Liverpool		

CHAPTER 31

"TEN MEN WON THE LEAGUE"

1978/79

The first half of the 1978/79 season was a funny one. There was no doubt that the country, while still retaining its reputation as the most football-loving country of them all, was suffering from a major collective hangover from Argentina in the summer of 1978. It was also the time when more and more people began to look at the facilities (an amazing number of grounds still had no Ladies toilets, for example), the moronic behaviour of some fans and to wonder whether football matches were really a good way of spending a Saturday afternoon. Football, generally in Scotland, had a major credibility problem.

Celtic had had a bad 12 months. The Dalglish transfer gifted Rangers the Treble in 1978 and had the major side effect of the departure of Jock Stein. Billy McNeill, who had had a good season as manager of Aberdeen in season 1977/78, was offered the job and took it. His arrival did give the fans a boost, but it would be a long time before the results did.

The first half of the 1978/79 season was a strange one, as no team managed to take a grip on Scottish football. Celtic's results were as quixotic and

Ecstasy at Celtic Park on 21 May 1979.

unpredictable as anyone else's. There had been a good start which included a win over Rangers at Celtic Park, but then inconsistency set in beginning with a defeat by Hibs at home, followed by awful performances at Aberdeen and Hearts with October being a particularly terrible month. A couple of days before Christmas, Celtic went down 0–1 to Morton at Cappielow. Bad weather prevented other games being played in the calendar year of 1978, and thus the curtain descended on the year of 1978 which many of us would choose to forget.

In addition to all this in the League, Celtic had fallen down in two other tournaments. One was the Anglo-Scottish Cup (a long-lost and little lamented tournament) in which Celtic lost to Burnley and the fans misbehaved into the bargain, and for the first time since 1963/64 they would not be in the Final of the Scottish League Cup, losing to Rangers in the semi-final in a strange game at Hampden in mid-December.

But it was not all that bad. There were three saving graces. One was that the fans did not turn on McNeill, giving him a chance and most importantly, time. Another was that, for his part, Billy McNeill had not been inactive, making two superb signings – Davie Provan from Kilmarnock and Murdo MacLeod from Dumbarton. Their impact would not be instantaneous, but it would be significant. And the third saving grace was that everyone else was in the same boat. Rangers were not having a good season either, and no team had taken a grip of things with Dundee United, Hearts, Aberdeen, Hibs, Partick Thistle and Morton all having their great moments but also their horrors. Everyone said that this was "good for Scottish football" but the attendances seemed to tell another tale.

1979 dawned with Celtic in sixth place but still within touching distance of League leaders Dundee United. In a sense, the League season had not really started yet, and indeed it would not really start until the month of March for there was an enforced "winter shut down" – the worst since 1963 – because of bad weather. Celtic's first League game of 1979 was against Aberdeen at Celtic Park on 3 March, although they had managed to play a couple of games in the Scottish Cup against Montrose and Berwick Rangers, two grounds which because of their proximity to the east coast evaded the worst of the weather.

The lay-off was probably a good thing, for it gave McNeill time to work with his hitherto underperforming squad and to introduce the new players, Provan and MacLeod, to the Celtic ethos. There was also the considerable, even the vital, added bonus of the return of Danny McGrain to the right-back spot.

It was a sunny, but windy day when Aberdeen came on 3 March. The pitch was far from ideal, but Alfie Conn scored the only goal of the game. It was a good start, but the same opponents put Celtic out of the Scottish Cup 11 days later. A couple of League victories followed but then the last day of March saw Celtic back to square one when, on the same depressing day that Rangers were winning the League Cup, Celtic went down to Hibs. When asked if Celtic looked like League winners, the BBC commentator answered baldly "No".

And yet there were still 14 games to go, and Celtic had no other commitments. "The Celts of old would have done it" said the veteran supporters, but frankly, the Celtic of 1979 was far from a vintage side. There was a further defeat at Tannadice on Wednesday 11 April, but this was a defeat that inspired Celtic, for it was a moral victory, and although Celtic fans left the ground fearing the worst about their League chances, there was, nevertheless, a feeling that things were slowly moving in the right direction.

By this time the League challengers had been whittled down to three – Celtic, Rangers and Dundee United, with United in the lead but having played more games than the other two. The games now came thick and fast in April, and a key game came on 28 April at Celtic Park against Dundee United. As a footballing spectacle, this was poor but Celtic edged home 2–1 with a fluky header from Johnny Doyle and a penalty from Andy Lynch. This game effectively ended Dundee United's stuttering title challenge, but there was still Rangers whom Celtic had to play twice.

The first game was at Hampden (Ibrox was under reconstruction) but it was a major disappointment, almost as bad as the victory of the Conservatives of Margaret Thatcher a couple of days previously in the 1979 general election. The 0–1 defeat was feckless and totally unpredictable following a very good 3–1 win over Hibs in midweek. This result gave Rangers a one-point advantage but it was still not the end of the world. Four games remained including the one against Rangers at Celtic Park, but shrewder supporters pointed out that the "other" games against Partick Thistle, St Mirren and Hearts were just as important.

Each one of these games was tight and tense (the St Mirren game was played at Ibrox on the Friday night before the Scottish Cup Final) but when the final whistle went after the 1–0 game over relegated Hearts (a truly awful game of football enlivened only by Mike Conroy's goal), Celtic knew that a win over Rangers on Monday, 21 May would win the League. Any other result would give the advantage to Rangers.

The stage was thus set for what is probably Celtic's third most famous game in our history (behind Lisbon and the 7–1) when 10 men won the League. The details are well known. Celtic were 0–1 down when Johnny Doyle was sent off for kicking a Rangers player who he thought was time wasting and faking an injury. It did not look good, but what this Celtic side lacked in skill, it made up for in spirit, and it was now that Roy Aitken took a grip of the game. Aitken scored, then crossed for McCluskey to put Celtic ahead. Rangers then equalised, but then came a piece of fortune when a ball bounced off defender Colin Jackson into the net. With time now running out, Murdo MacLeod then added a fourth with a shot that he reckoned would go into the Celtic end and time would be wasted before it came back. But he scored, and bedlam and mayhem took over Celtic Park.

What a shame that the game was not televised or on the radio! It was, however, a glorious triumph for Billy McNeill in his first year of management. Classy football was not seen very often that season, but there was no lack of passion or determination to fight back from adversity.

Other tournaments were as follows:

Scottish Cup Final		
Rangers 3 Hibs 2	Hampden	28 May
(after two 0-0 draws on 12 and 16 May at Hampden)		
Scottish League Cup Final		
Rangers 2 Aberdeen 1	Hampden	31 March
English Cup Final		
Arsenal 3 Manchester United 2	Wembley	12 May
English League Cup Final		
Nottingham Forest 3 Southampton 2	Wembley	17 March
English League		
Liverpool		

CHAPTER 32

HAPPY DAYS

1980/81

Celtic's failure to land the Scottish League in 1980 sat ill with the support. Apparently in a strong position and lulled into a false sense of security by a respectable performance against Real Madrid in the European Cup, then a win over Rangers at the beginning of April, Celtic had then managed to lose twice to Aberdeen at Celtic Park and made two awful trips to Tayside to lose to the Dundee teams. It was shockingly unprofessional and although the Scottish Cup won in the "riot" Final against Rangers provided some solace, 1980 was a bitter summer.

But the chastened McNeill brought in two significant players at the start of the season. One was the Irish goalkeeper Pat Bonner who had been around for a while without breaking through, and the other was a supremely talented young man by the name of Charlie Nicholas. Both were instant successes and very popular with the support, but it would be some time before the team settled into any kind of consistent form.

Autumn 1980 was not a great time. An early exit from Europe at the hands of some little-known Eastern Europeans, defeat in the League Cup at the hands of Dundee United and two successive League defeats in early November to Rangers and then Aberdeen meant that things were not looking too good with questions being asked about whether Billy McNeill was really managerial material. It was often said of Billy that he was too much of a supporter to be a great manager and he certainly did get overemotional at times. Now, one wondered about his repeated failures against Alex Ferguson of Aberdeen and Jim McLean of Dundee United, two teams who had now emerged to be called the "New Firm". On the other hand, these teams tended to play boring, defensive football, something that the Celtic tradition would simply not allow.

Sometimes Celtic did indeed turn it on. They beat Dundee United 3–0 at Tannadice at the end of November, but then a reasonable run of form in December (admittedly against none too demanding opposition in Partick Thistle, Hearts and Airdrie) was brought to a halt by a comprehensive 1–4 defeat at Pittodrie in the last game of 1980. It was a hard pitch, but Celtic were frankly outplayed, being 0–4 down before Charlie Nicholas managed to pull one back. Celtic were now three points behind Aberdeen and had played one extra game. Things looked bad. Yet there was one positive aspect for Celtic, and that

"Cheeky Charlie" in his prime.

was that the supporters stayed loyal and frankly out shouted the home support in their defiance. They had been through a great deal of heartbreak in 1980, and in spite of all their mutterings about Billy's leadership and the slightly more strongly expressed reservations about the stewardship of the club at board level, they were still showing that they supported the concept of Celtic.

They got their reward in 1981. It was as if Billy McNeill had suddenly pressed a button, and the light went on. It was not that there was any great change in personnel, although Roddie MacDonald, who had been struggling for a time, was given a back seat, Dom Sullivan was deployed in midfield a lot more, and a young left-back called Mark Reid began to impress. The big difference, however, was that so many players – Roy Aitken, Tommy Burns and Frank McGarvey, for example – whom we had known for some time had the ability, now began to show it on a consistent basis. And there was also Charlie Nicholas! One or two journalists used the word "Pele" to compare him with, whereas a veteran supporter went one better – he likened Charlie Nicholas to Patsy Gallacher!

The great thing about the form of early 1981 was that it improved gradually gaining momentum as it moved along. New Year's Day at Kilmarnock saw an early reverse but then a spirited fightback and a 2–1 victory which was welcome, although hardly inspiring. Two good home victories followed over Morton and Dundee United, and then at the end of January came a very good 3–0 win over Hearts at Tynecastle on a day when Rangers beat Aberdeen at Ibrox, a result which helped Celtic. Celtic's position at the top of the League was confirmed on 7 February without kicking a ball. Their game at Partick Thistle was off (strangely, for conditions did not look all that bad) and both Aberdeen and Rangers lost to their two respective bogey teams, Morton and Dundee United.

From now on, Celtic never looked back. The game against Rangers on 21 February was won with a great deal more ease than the 3–1 scoreline would suggest, Morton were then competently dispatched on the last day of February and then two weeks after that came one of Celtic's best performance of recent years when they beat St Mirren 7–0 at Celtic Park. The football was absolutely scintillating, and Frank McGarvey managed to score a hat-trick before half-time! Words like "devastating" were freely used, and as often happens when Celtic are doing well, their opponents, miles away, almost sense what is going on and "blow up", as it were! Both Aberdeen and Rangers lost that day, further strengthening Celtic's position at the top.

Aberdeen's last real chance came at Celtic Park on 28 March. It was a game they really had to win, and they were 1–0 up for a long spell, until Celtic proved that they were worthy of the League flag with a devastating second-half display in which they earned a draw. Indeed, it would have been a comfortable win if Murdo MacLeod had made a better job of a penalty kick or if the Jungle side linesman had not disallowed a perfectly good George McCluskey goal. But a draw was enough for Celtic to retain their comfortable lead at the top of the League.

Three League wins now followed – a 6–0 thrashing of Hearts, a tight 1–0 win at Firhill on a Sunday and then a 1–0 win over Rangers at Ibrox, the goal coming from the effervescent Charlie Nicholas whose form had shown no sign of tapering off. All this meant that Celtic could win the League with a draw in a rearranged game against Dundee United at Tannadice on Wednesday, 22 April.

These games were always close and interesting, and this time spice had been added by the fact that the previous midweek Dundee United had beaten Celtic in the replayed semi-final of the Scottish Cup. (A major reason for that may have been the absence through injury of Danny McGrain.) This had been a major disappointment for Celtic, and had also been a major reversal of roles, for Dundee United seldom won in Glasgow. Now Celtic were being asked to win the Scottish League in Dundee! But crucially, McGrain was back.

It was a very cold night with snow showers around, but Celtic fans turned up in strength clearly infiltrating the "home support" section. Murdo MacLeod scored in the second minute, and then after United equalised, McGarvey scored again before half-time and then in the second half we saw one of the best goals that Tommy Burns ever scored into the "Shed" end of the ground. Dundee United pulled one back, but Celtic held out comfortably for a famous win, and the night finished with the Celtic players "chairing" their captain Danny McGrain and manager Billy McNeill round the ground.

The rest of the season had been disappointing, but the League season was a total success. McNeill's popularity had been reinstated, and the future looked bright. It would be nice to see a European campaign again, and that seemed a distinct possibility with the players at McNeill's disposal. Significantly, they were all playing with an obvious desire to play for Celtic, and that is always something that counts for a great deal with the support.

Scottish Cup Final		
Rangers 4 Dundee United 1	Hampden	12 May
(after 0-0 draw at Hampden on 9 May)		
Scottish League Cup Final		
Dundee United 3 Dundee 0	Dens Park	6 December
English Cup Final		
Tottenham Hotspur 3 Manchester City 2	Wembley	14 May
(after 1-1 draw at Wembley on 9 May)		
English League Cup Final		
Liverpool 2 West Ham United 1	Villa Park	1 April
(after 1-1 draw at Wembley on 14 March)		
English League		
Aston Villa		

CHAPTER 33

ANOTHER SOLID TRIUMPH

1981/82

Celtic retained their title in 1982. Like 1981, it was a season bereft of glory in other tournaments, but Celtic won this League Championship basically through their ability to graft and to grind out victories. This time they faced a stronger challenge from Aberdeen, and it was Aberdeen who put them out of the Scottish Cup in February. Once again Rangers failed to maintain the pace and had dropped out of the title race long before the nerve wracking final day. They were, however, involved in it, as we shall see.

Charlie Nicholas played only a few games this season, having sustained a serious injury. He was badly missed but on the other hand, towards the end of the season, another great player appeared. This was Paul McStay, a youngster who had starred in a televised game of the Scotland Schoolboys in 1980 and had since developed at a fast pace. Another factor of this season – and it rather distorted things – was the bad weather in December and January from which Celtic seemed to suffer more than others.

Celtic started the season very badly and having lost their first two sectional games in the League Cup, never really recovered in that competition. They also exited Europe at the first time of asking, losing to Juventus in Turin after a reasonable performance at Celtic Park. Their bogey team this year was Hibs – an odd one that! – for Celtic lost twice at Easter Road – and dropped a point at Celtic Park in February. Another feature of this campaign was the

Danny McGrain with the League Championship trophy on the shoulders of Roy Aitken and with Davie Provan and George McCluskey in the picture.

very low attendances. Other than games against Rangers and Aberdeen, Celtic Park rarely housed crowds of more than 20,000. Clearly, the Dalglish transfer of 1977 still bit deep and hurt viscerally.

In spite of disappointments in other tournaments, Celtic started the League campaign very well, and September saw good victories at Pittodrie and Ibrox. Frank McGarvey and George McCluskey were in among the goals, Roy Aitken, Tommy Burns and Murdo MacLeod were a superb midfield and Celtic were an entertaining team to watch. When they did slip up in successive weeks in October, they had reason to complain about refereeing decisions. Dundee United scored in the first minute at Celtic Park with a goal that had been blatantly hand-balled. That was the first dropped point of the season, and then next week at Easter Road Hibs got a soft penalty. Yet Celtic could hardly complain, for they too got a penalty and missed it – to the delight of Hibs manager Bertie Auld.

But the disappointment was short-lived, because Celtic then beat Aberdeen again, this time at Celtic Park, then drew a very exciting game with Rangers at Parkhead 3–3. Young Davie Moyes impressed in this game, and it was certainly great entertainment, although it possibly highlighted the fact that Celtic's defence was slightly more fallible than it might have been. The last League game of 1981 took place on 5 December – a competent 3–1 defeat of Dundee – for after that the snow and the frost came down and very few games were played in Scotland in the rest of December with many clubs, including Celtic, worried about lack of income creating a cash-flow problem.

But for once Rangers had stolen a march on Celtic. As well as building a new stadium which was, frankly, well ahead of anyone else's, they had also installed an under-soil central heating system which allowed the Old Firm derby on 9 January to go ahead. It being Celtic's first real game for over a month, they were, not surprisingly, rather rusty and lost 0–1 to a Rangers team who were only marginally better. Nevertheless, Rangers had pointed the way forward with their under-soil heating system, and although it would take some time for that particular penny to drop at Celtic Park, it did eventually happen.

The weather eased by the end of January, and Celtic delighted their fans with a great display at Aberdeen in a 3–1 win, a game in which Paul McStay scored a great goal and began to show what a great player he was going to become. Yet no sooner had the afterglow of this great and significant victory subsided than the Hibs complex struck in the shape of a feckless 0–0 draw at Parkhead on the Wednesday night. This game was marked by a partial floodlight failure, but the game continued nevertheless. It might have been better if it hadn't! Then at the end of the month Bertie Auld once again got the better of Billy McNeill when Hibs beat Celtic 1–0 at Easter Road.

As Celtic had also gone out of the Scottish Cup in mid-February, it was not a great time for Celtic, although their good start meant that they were still reasonably comfortable at the top. They became a little less so when Aberdeen at last beat

Celtic in a League match at the end of March, a narrow 0–1 game which featured a very lucky goal for Aberdeen and yet again a missed penalty (a recurring theme) by Celtic. Celtic immediately redeemed themselves however when Tommy Burns scored two great goals to beat Dundee United at Tannadice the following midweek, a game marred by a broken leg for Frank McGarvey.

At this point International affairs intervened when Argentina invaded the Falkland Islands and Britain retaliated. It was a difficult one this for Celtic supporters. They were no lovers of Mrs Thatcher, or indeed of Great Britain; on the other hand, the Argentinian government was a viciously repressive Fascist "tin pot junta", as a Labour politician called them. While the House of Commons met in emergency session and Scottish Cup semi-finals were being played, Celtic played a disappointing 1–1 draw at Morton, something which meant that Celtic would now only be three points ahead of Aberdeen, and that was with the proviso that Celtic won their games in hand. And because of the bad weather in the winter, there were still nine games left for a nervous Celtic to negotiate.

But the rest of April was good for Celtic. A win over Rangers at Parkhead was followed by four wins on the trot over Airdrie at Broomfield, the two Dundee teams at Parkhead and then Partick Thistle at the always tricky venue of Firhill. Aberdeen in the meantime were still pressing, although their challenge seemed to be fatally impaired by a last-minute defeat at their bogey ground of Cappielow. On 1 May, Celtic at last laid low their Hibs complex by thrashing them 6–0 on a day punctuated by hail showers.

All this meant that two points would win the League for Celtic. Three games remained, two of them at home against St Mirren who had had a good season and would finish fifth, the other away to Dundee United. They got one of the two points against St Mirren on the Holiday Monday of 3 May in a rather unsatisfactory performance, but then chose to put on one of their worst performances for many years when they lost to Dundee United 0–3 at Tannadice.

Scottish Cup Final		
Aberdeen 4 Rangers 1	Hampden	22 May
Scottish League Cup Final		
Rangers 2 Dundee United 1	Hampden	28 November
English Cup Final		
Tottenham Hotspur 1 Manchester City 0 (after 1-1 draw at Wembley on 22 May)	Wembley	27 May
English League Cup Final		
Liverpool 3 Tottenham Hotspur 2 aet	Wembley	13 March
English League		
Liverpool		

The best interpretation was to put it all down to "nerves", but it meant that Celtic could, after all, lose the League if they lost to St Mirren at Parkhead and Aberdeen beat Rangers 5–0 at Pittodrie. A nervous first half at Celtic Park was followed by the disturbing news that Aberdeen were 4–0 up over Rangers. It was probably not true that Rangers were "lying down" (Aberdeen would beat them 4–1 next week in the Scottish Cup Final, and Rangers themselves had struggled to beat Forfar Athletic in the semi-final) but it meant that Celtic had to score and beat St Mirren. Incredibly, some Celtic fans were shouting for the Dons to "pile them on", but the general atmosphere was one of tension until George McCluskey, Tom McAdam and then George McCluskey scored again to beat the Buddies and bring home the League title for the 33rd time.

CHAPTER 34

ALBERT KIDD

1985/86

Season 1985/86 was a remarkable one in Scottish football. The early part of the season was dominated by the death of Jock Stein on the bench at the end of the Wales v. Scotland World Cup qualifier, and then by Scotland's prolonged and eventually successful campaign (which took them to Australia) to qualify for the World Cup finals. It was also a year which saw a dispute between the SFA, the Scottish League and the TV companies which meant no football, not even recorded highlights, until a spectacular kissing and making up which led to some Scottish League games being shown live – a decision which would have made many administrators of previous eras turn in their graves!

Not to put too fine a point on it, Celtic in the early part of the season were poor. It was a source of mystery why so many talented players – Paul McStay, Murdo MacLeod, Tommy Burns, to name but a few – could not take charge of the League and win it by the veritable country mile. But inconsistency was the order of the day – there was a particular run in October/November when four games out of five were lost and all to the title challengers of Hearts, Dundee United, Aberdeen and Rangers, and fingers began to be pointed at Davie Hay, the amiable manager who seemed to be struggling with the demands of the job.

The Scottish League Cup had been lost in the unlucky circumstances of a penalty shoot-out at Easter Road, the European campaign never survived the first hurdle of Atletico Madrid, and the League campaign was floundering. It was a depressing time to be a Celtic supporter, but some mirth was created with the appearance of Hearts in the list of Championship contenders. At first it seemed to be a joke inspired by the writers of the Edinburgh-based *Scotsman* newspaper, but a run of good results made the world take this team seriously. They had seemed to be in danger of becoming a yo-yo team with their frequent relegations of recent years but now under Alec McDonald and Sandy Jardine, one time of Rangers, were putting together a decent run of results.

As early as the first day of the season Hearts had been clearly the better team against Celtic at Tynecastle, and Celtic had needed a last-minute Paul McStay goal, a miskick which apologetically hit the post and trundled in, to earn a 1–1 draw which honest supporters admitted was lucky. (It would be a long time before the significance of that goal was understood!) Hearts' good form in midwinter had been aided by the fact that not only were Celtic

Albert Kidd, Dundee FC.

struggling (two dreadful defeats at Tannadice Park to Dundee United on either side of the New Year, for example) but so too were the others. Rangers were, if anything worse than Celtic (Celtic beat them on New Year's Day), Aberdeen were inconsistent, and Dundee United, always a difficult team on their own soil, could be relied upon to obey the apparently immutable law that they were not allowed to do so well away from home.

Celtic drew 1–1 at Parkhead with Aberdeen on 11 January – an appalling day of wind and rain – and a glance at the League table showed that Celtic were fifth. Things did not look good, but a closer glance would reveal that they were only six points behind leaders Hearts, and they had games in hand. Loads of games remained, although we were past the halfway stage, and the League was still there for the taking. Indeed, the newspapers and the radio stations were purring their pleasure about how "open" and "competitive" it all was. It was a shame that the ongoing TV dispute prevented the punters from seeing it!

Celtic's unimpressive form continued, but then came Hearts' visit to Celtic Park on 22 February. To their credit, Hearts filled most of the Rangers end, and a great game ensued before 45,366 fans on a very cold day with goals from John Robertson and Murdo MacLeod making it a creditable 1–1 draw. Celtic then went out of the Scottish Cup to Hibs, drew disappointingly with Dundee United at Parkhead, and then on 22 March took part in the famous 4–4 draw at Ibrox, described by some journalists (with a hint of hyperbole) as the "best Old Firm game of all time". The defending was deplorable in the wet conditions, Willie McStay got a red card, the entertainment was good, and in some ways the game was the catalyst for Celtic's charge for the flag in that it seemed to give them some confidence that had, apparently, been lacking hitherto. Hearts had beaten Hibs that day and were now seven points ahead of Celtic, although Celtic had two games in hand.

But with the weather now improving, Celtic suddenly began to win games. Clydebank were dispatched 5–0, then difficult games against Dundee and St Mirren were negotiated before the vital win at Pittodrie on 12 April, where a Mo Johnston goal was enough to damage, irreparably, Aberdeen's chances. But Hearts were still five points ahead, albeit with one extra game played. Celtic gained a little the following weekend. They beat Hibs 2–0 on the Saturday, then on the Sunday in Scotland's first ever live televising of a League game (to seal the new deal) Hearts dropped a point to Aberdeen at Tynecastle.

Four points and a game in hand! The next two Saturdays, Celtic won – but so did Hearts. Then on Wednesday, 30 April, Celtic played off their game in hand at Motherwell and won 2–0, a slightly disappointing scoreline, for more goals appeared to have been required. Nevertheless, Celtic still had an outside chance of the title if they hammered St Mirren by at least four goals at Love Street, and Hearts lost to Dundee at Dens Park.

It didn't appear likely. All Hearts had to do on the fateful day of 3 May was draw against a Dundee team that was competent but no more than that. But Hearts had looked for a few weeks like a man on his way to the dentist's, apprehensive and edgy. They would claim later that there was a "virus" in their camp. Not everyone believed that, although university students before their final exams are often known to suffer from a "virus", usually of the psychological or psychosomatic variety. This may have happened here as the strain of not having won the League since 1960 began to tell. Meanwhile, Edinburgh outfitters began to sell loads of Hearts scarves for the Johnny-come-latelies who had been nowhere in sight when they got relegated.

Radio told everyone at Dens Park that Celtic were winning 4–0 at half-time with some tremendous goals. They scored another soon after, but all that Hearts had to do was draw. John Robertson and John Colquhoun had reasonable chances, but frayed nerves played a part, and the Hearts fans behind that Tannadice end of Dens Park were now looking at watches and counting down to full-time. They did look like holding out, but decades of awful Tynecastle teams had taught the Gorgie supporters not to get too uppity. Yet celebrations had already been planned...

But then late in the second half, on came the Angel of Death in the unlikely shape of Albert Kidd. It would be a fair bet that no one in the Hearts support (nor the Celtic support, for that matter) had heard of Albert. His career with Dundee had been mediocre to disappointing (to put it tactfully) so far, but there are times that Destiny calls. Crucially, Albert, like so many Dundonians, was Celtic daft and he may also have felt that if his professional career was to go anywhere, it had to be today.

Today it was! Two goals, the second one an absolute stormer through a Hearts defence who had already sensed that the game was up, won the League for Celtic, the radio bringing the glad tidings to Love Street where some of the Celtic fans had already gone home to get out of the rain, and to

Scottish Cup Final		
Aberdeen 3 Hearts 0	Hampden	10 May
Scottish League Cup Final		
Aberdeen 3 Hibs 0	Hampden	27 October
English Cup Final		
Liverpool 3 Everton 1	Wembley	10 May
English League Cup Final		
Oxford United 3 QPR 0	Wembley	20 April
English League		
Liverpool		

Murdo MacLeod.

Easter Road, while at Ibrox (where they are never too bright at the best of times) consternation reigned for they thought that the goals had been scored by Walter Kidd who played for Hearts.

No one could say that Celtic necessarily left everyone standing that season. In fact, there was an element of luck about the 34th triumph, but no one could deny that it was one of the most exciting ends to the season that one could imagine, and how everyone celebrated at Love Street, singing the praises of a new hero called Albert Kidd! Hearts now sentenced their fans to even more misery by losing the Scottish Cup Final as well in a dismal surrender to Aberdeen.

CHAPTER 35

CENTENARY CELEBRATIONS

1987/88

Celtic are, thank goodness, a team who are always very conscious of their own history. This is how it should be and one hopes that it will continue. 1987/88 was the Centenary Season, and although pedants could argue over when Celtic were founded (6 November 1887, to be exact) and when they played their first game (28 May 1888), it mattered not, for they were both encompassed in this season. The 50th Anniversary of 1938 had been well celebrated with the Empire Exhibition Trophy and Scottish League of that year. It would be nice, it was felt, if 1988 could be similarly celebrated.

1986/87 had not been a great season. The League had been thrown away after Celtic had been well in front, and four players – Maurice Johnston, Brian McClair, Murdo MacLeod and Alan McInally – had left in the summer. So too had manager Davie Hay. He had been shown the door, but the supporters were greatly enthused by the news that Billy McNeill was coming back. Since his sad and unnecessary departure in 1983, Billy had spent several fruitless years with Manchester City and Aston Villa, but there had been little doubt where he wanted to be. Sometimes on radio interviews when asked about Celtic, he gave himself away by saying "we".

"We" certainly needed him, for the brutal professionalism of Graeme Souness' hired mercenaries was now apparent. "Win at all costs" seemed to be the watchword, and the bullying of opponents and referees was sometimes quite frightening to behold. It did, tragically, seem to work as Celtic (and the other teams) withered away in front of them. McNeill's remit was to stop that. McNeill's first tenure of office had been characterised by his shrewd and astute signings. He did the same again. Mick McCarthy had already been bought by David Hay, but McNeill brought in Andy Walker, Chris Morris, Billy Stark, Joe Miller and Frank McAvennie, all of whom played a significant part in the centenary season.

There were the usual early exits from Europe and the Scottish League Cup, but in this case, it merely cleared the ground for the Scottish League. There was an early season defeat at Dunfermline, a few disappointing draws and another defeat by Dundee United, but after the end of October, with all the signings in place, the team settled down to a rich vein of form and did not lose again until the League was more or less won.

Celtic had beaten Rangers at Celtic Park on 29 August – Graeme Souness being sent off for a tackle on Billy Stark

Victorian Celts? No, closer inspection will reveal that these two gentlemen are in fact Roy Aitken and Paul McStay celebrating Celtic's Centenary.

after Stark's boot had come off (you couldn't make that one up, could you?) – and the game at Ibrox in October became a cause celebre in Scottish legal circles when McAvennie and two Rangers ended up in court, for something, that in all honesty, could have been dealt with within football rather than involving the judiciary – and wasn't all that bad in any case!

The League was a large one this season with 12 teams, and 44 games were necessary, so fixtures had to be arranged on funny days. Thus, on either side of Christmas two games were played at traditionally difficult grounds for Celtic – Brockville where Celtic beat Falkirk 2–0, one of the goals being a marvellous one from Paul McStay, and then on Boxing Day at Tannadice where Celtic laid a few bogeys when Joe Miller scored a late winner.

And so Rangers came on 2 January. This game may not necessarily have won the League for Celtic, but it certainly put them in the driving seat, both in terms of points advantage and also in the psychological factor. Celtic were simply so far ahead of Rangers that day and worth a great deal more than the 2–0 win which Frank McAvennie's goals bestowed on a delirious Parkhead.

The important thing was now for Billy McNeill to keep his players' feet on the ground and get them to concentrate on the important task of simply winning games. There was the recent precedent of last year when a substantial lead had been thrown away. Not this year, however. There were a few wobbles in the shape of draws at St Mirren on a difficult pitch on 9 January and a dull draw against a Dundee United side at Parkhead on 26 March when the Tannadice team bus seemed to have joined the Dundee United defence in the penalty box! There was also a game against Morton at Parkhead in late February which ended up a victory but only through a very generous late penalty which the crowd didn't even claim for!

Against that, however, there were some very fine performances. A win over Dundee at Dens Park on a windy day in mid-February was sealed by a late Frank McAvennie header, Dunfermline were taken apart in a 4–0 defeat on Wednesday night in early March, then that win was consolidated by a competent performance against Falkirk before we came to what was generally reckoned to be Rangers' last chance. It was a televised game at Ibrox on Sunday, 20 March. The game was close and better behaved than some recent encounters but Celtic won 2–1, with the whole nation now seeing the value of Paul McStay not only in his general play throughout but particularly in his terrific goal from the edge of the penalty box.

Then Celtic went to two difficult venues of Pittodrie and Easter Road and won at both places. At Pittodrie on Wednesday, 30 March, Andy Walker scored Celtic's goal in the 1–0 win which was far from simple, but three days later at Easter Road, they had it a little easier with goals from Peter Grant and Andy Walker. Beating St Mirren 2–0 at Parkhead the following midweek meant that the title could be sealed at Tynecastle on 16 April.

Celtic had put Hearts out of the Scottish Cup the week before, and this time there was grim determination in the ranks of the Jambos for some revenge. They got it, and much was made of the fact that Celtic could not celebrate in front of them. Those people, however, who see "conspiracy" in such results looked at the crowd next week at Celtic Park for the visit of Dundee and nodded sagely or said "I told you so".

The crowd on 23 April was given as 60,800. It was later admitted to be 72,000 but even that looked a conservative estimate as Celtic fans were allowed to enter the section reserved for away support and also allowed to sit round the running track. The main stand was full and closed at 1.30 p.m. for a 3.00 p.m. kick-off! It was quite clearly Britain's biggest crowd of the season, and even at that, there were thousands locked outside, compelled to listen to the radio commentary and envying those who had got there in loads of time. But inside, the sheer size of the crowd was terrifying.

The underrated full-back Chris Morris scored in the early stages for Celtic, and then in the second half Andy Walker scored twice within a minute to put the game well out of Dundee's reach and to land Celtic's 35th League Championship as the crowd celebrated their Centenary by singing "Happy Birthday". It was a great Celtic occasion. Symbolically, the sun came out near the end of the game (it had been a dull day up to then) as if to join in the celebrations. "God is a Celtic supporter", said the lady beside me.

Much credit was rightly given to Billy McNeill who had brought such glory to the club. Three weeks later the Scottish Cup was won as well, and everything looked so rosy. One knows that the fans enjoyed themselves that summer. There was much to be happy about in the shape of a Celtic Musical on in Glasgow and loads of beds of green and white flowers at the Glasgow Garden Festival of that year. Sadly, it would not last – and the bad days were fast approaching. 1988 was great, though!

Scottish Cup Final		
Celtic 2 Dundee United 1	Hampden	14 May
Scottish League Cup Final		
Rangers 3 Aberdeen 3	Hampden	25 October
(Rangers won 5-3 on penalties)		
English Cup Final		
Wimbledon 1 Liverpool 0	Wembley	14 May
English League Cup Final		
Luton Town 3 Arsenal 2	Wembley	24 April
English League		
Liverpool		

CHAPTER 36

BREAKING THE CHAINS

1997/98

Supporting Celtic in the 1990s was no joke. Words almost fail the historian as he tries to catalogue everything that went wrong in those devastating years. No one could have guessed in 1988 that a whole decade of horror was about to unfold. Everyone knew that not everything was right at Celtic Park at director level in 1998, but few did not believe that it couldn't be righted with a few adjustments to the demands of the 1990s. Sadly, we were mistaken, and in 1994, in circumstances that remind one of the Russian Revolution of 1917, the old regime fell. Fortunately no blood was actually shed, but there was a copious amount of pain.

The rebuilding of the team began in 1994. It took time, but the Scottish Cup was won in 1995, seen as a sort of stepping stone to League success. Celtic ought to have won the League in 1996 and might have done so in 1997 as well had they not been handicapped by some emotionally instable players who claimed their love for Celtic, but frankly did not understand what the concept of Celtic meant.

Tommy Burns was sacked in 1997 and replaced by a little-known curly-haired Dutchman called Wim Jansen who had been in the Feyenoord team which beat Celtic in the European Cup Final of 1970. There was also an appointment of a

Wim Jansen and Murdo MacLeod show off the League Championship trophy.

General Manager or Director of Football in Jock Brown, a good TV commentator. He was also a lawyer and would, presumably, be good at negotiating for new players. Celtic bought in a few players whom no one had heard of – a chap called Larsson, for example – but everyone approached the 1997/98 season with dread, fearing that Rangers might win 10 League titles in a row.

The beginning was catastrophic. A defeat to Hibs at Easter Road was followed by another at Parkhead against an incredulous Dunfermline, and it might even have been three in a row at St Johnstone, but for a brilliant diving header from Henrik Larsson as Celtic registered their first win of the season. Slowly things began to improve, although the European tie against Liverpool came just too early for the new developing Celts.

There were wins over Motherwell, Aberdeen, Dundee United, Kilmarnock and Hearts before we came to the rather significant month of November. Because of the death (many Celtic supporters used the word "murder" in this context) of Diana, Princess of Wales in late August, the authorities had been bullied into postponing the Old Firm fixture. Thus Celtic played Rangers twice in November. One was a depressing 0–1 defeat at Ibrox, followed by an even sadder performance against Motherwell at Celtic Park which saw Regi Blinker sent off in a 0–2 defeat, but then things were partially restored when a late Alan Stubbs header got Celtic a draw in the postponed Rangers game at Parkhead. It was only a draw, but had it not been for that draw, it would have been difficult to envisage Celtic winning the League that year.

But then came the important psychological winning of the Scottish League Cup at Ibrox at the end of the month. It was only Celtic's second trophy of the 1990s (an indication of how far we had sunk) but the victory over Dundee United showed that we could win something, and we then had some good wins in December over Aberdeen, Hearts and Hibs before finishing 1997 on a low note. On the Saturday between Christmas and New Year at McDiarmid Park, Celtic, without Henrik Larsson, battered the St Johnstone defence but could not get a goal and went down 0–1.

As the year turned, there was a genuine interest throughout Scotland and indeed the world in this League campaign. In fact, it was a three-horse race, for Hearts were involved as well, even leading on occasion, and some Celtic fans were even heard in their moments of weakness to say that they would actually settle for Hearts becoming champions to stop this dreaded phrase called "ten in a row". It was a momentary madness, however, for on 2 January, Celtic beat Rangers 2–0 with two great goals from two signings of 1997, Craig Burley and Paul Lambert, Lambert in particular proving to be a great acquisition for the team.

Celtic, however, were still behind, albeit marginally, and there was a long way to go. However, there was now a consistency about the team with the occasional brilliant performance. On 21 February, for example, Harald Brattbakk, that much maligned and ridiculed Norwegian, suddenly turned it on and scored all four goals as Celtic beat Kilmarnock 4–0, and it should have been more! There was an agreeable ability to beat Aberdeen, Dunfermline and Hibs, but there were a couple of disappointments in March when we failed to beat Dundee United and Hearts at Parkhead. The Dundee United game, a televised Sunday occasion, was remarkable. Celtic were 1–0 up in the first half and completely on top before unaccountably letting United back in. Two weeks after that, the 0–0 draw against Hearts was simply 90 minutes of barely any football at all, and March ended with Celtic, Rangers and Hearts all locked together at the top.

The situation was not helped by the news emanating from Parkhead about contracts, and the clear impression that Wim Jansen and Jock Brown did not very often go out for a pint together. Oh dear! Was the Celtic self-destruction impulse (a strong and ever present motif in the 1990s) going to hit us yet again and cause permanent damage to the memory of Jock Stein's great sides? Were Rangers going to be able to claim that they were better than the Celtic teams of that blessed era?

Things now got a great deal worse when we lost to Rangers on successive Sundays, once in the Scottish Cup and once in the League. Although there had been a good win at Rugby Park, Kilmarnock between those games, the reverse at Ibrox meant that with four games left, Celtic and Rangers (Hearts were by now slowly disappearing from the scene) were equal on points but Rangers had a marginally better goal difference. The four remaining League games were indeed to be "four Cup Finals".

The footballing world was now enthralled with most neutral opinion siding with Celtic (for they had had enough of the arrogant Rangers) and everyone seemed to be talking about little else. The press tended to side with Rangers, but the level of sheer trash and drivel meant that it was becoming increasingly difficult to take newspapers seriously.

Celtic, however, went ahead on the weekend of 18/19 April. A 4–1 win over Motherwell was good in itself, but then the following day at Pittodrie, TV viewers saw Aberdeen (who had had a poor season) suddenly rise to the occasion and beat Rangers, a club that their fans, players and officials had always detested. "We hate Rangers more than you" their fans shouted to Celtic fans on occasion, although they were probably wrong there!

Celtic were now three points ahead, but then infuriated the support by only drawing 0–0 against relegation-threatened Hibs at Parkhead. It was a performance that deservedly brought the wrath of the support on the players, but it was not yet a disaster, for although Rangers beat Hearts at Tynecastle, Celtic were still that one point ahead as the penultimate weekend approached – Rangers entertaining Kilmarnock at Ibrox on Saturday, and Celtic at Dunfermline on TV on Sunday.

This was the weekend that two totally insignificant characters earned their brief moments of glory. Ally Mitchell of Kilmarnock scored the only goal, late in the game, at Ibrox which would have allowed Celtic the chance to win the League at Dunfermline the following day. But we could only draw, thwarted by

Wim Jansen and Fergus McCann.

a curious headed goal by a gentleman called Craig Faulconbridge.

And so to that final day. The intervening week was full of tension, psychosomatic illnesses, insomnia and recurrent nightmares about mass suicides by punters jumping from the high stands at Celtic Park. St Johnstone's manager Paul Sturrock apparently received death threats from crackpots of both persuasions, but there was little doubt that the Perth men were enjoying their moment in the limelight, as indeed were Dundee United who could yet win the title for Celtic if they beat or even drew with Rangers at Tannadice.

The Jock Stein Stand at Celtic Park had not yet been built and the crowd was restricted to 49,000. But there were almost as many Celtic fans outside the ground as there were in it, listening to the roar of the crowd and transistor radios. Fortunately it all turned out well – Henrik Larsson early on and Harald Brattbakk in the latter stages, triggering off the greatest party that the Celtic support had enjoyed for many, many years. But the predominant emotion was relief!

There were two postscripts. One was that Wim Jansen did indeed fall on his sword and depart – but we were all grateful to him for his professionalism in seeing the League campaign through – and the other was that the following week, Hearts ended their trophy famine which had lasted since 1962 by beating Rangers at Celtic Park to lift the Scottish Cup. It is not often that we cheer the Jambos, but we were so relaxed, happy and satisfied in any case. The horror days were over. Celtic were back!

Scottish Cup Final		
Hearts 2 Rangers 1	Celtic Park	16 May
Scottish League Cup Final		
Celtic 3 Dundee United 0	Ibrox	30 November
English Cup Final		
Arsenal 2 Newcastle United 0	Wembley	16 May
English League Cup Final		
Chelsea 2 Middlesbrough 0	Wembley	29 March
English League		
Arsenal		

CHAPTER 37

O'NEILL AND LARSSON

2000/01

Celtic teetered on the brink of another crisis in summer 2000. Since Jansen's unfortunate departure in 1998, things had not been so good. Jo Venglos was possibly too old and certainly did not understand Celtic and Scotland well enough to be a success, and John Barnes had simply been a disaster. He had been sacked after the Inverness fiasco of February 2000 and matters were left in the hands of Kenny Dalglish, who had indeed won Celtic the Scottish League Cup in March but who had failed to make any real impact on the Scottish League.

Celtic could not afford another managerial flop, but this time at last they got it right in the appointment of the talented but sometimes apparently humourless and inscrutable Martin O'Neill. Not only that, but the board also decided to back him with cash and O'Neill had been around English football for long enough to know what a good player was as Chris Sutton, Alan Thompson, Neil Lennon and others arrived to provide the long overdue challenge to Rangers, who had been allowed to get off with far too much for far too long.

The League season opened at Tannadice Park in late July against Dundee United, who had rather upstaged Celtic by wearing green jerseys! It mattered not, for Celtic won 2–1. The next two home games against Motherwell and Kilmarnock were little to write home about, but they were wins, but it was the last two games of August which set the tone for the season. First Hearts were defeated at Tynecastle and that was good enough, but then came the still famous 6–2 win over Rangers in which Celtic were three up before 15 minutes had been played, Fernando Ricksen was taken off before half-time, Henrik Larsson scored one of his best ever goals in the second half and then Barry Ferguson saw a red card.

Paul Lambert with Martin O'Neill.

It was a game which, in more senses than one, knocked Rangers for six, and it was the day that the immortal "And the cry was no defenders..." was born. From now on, Celtic simply took charge and did not drop a point until 1 October at Pittodrie, with Henrik Larsson in particular showing the world that he had recovered totally from his broken leg of last season, and that he was one of the best goalscorers in world football.

The other effect that the 6–2 game had was that it galvanised the Celtic support who now began to attend in great numbers and to fill the ground every home game as Celtic beat Hibs, Dundee, St Mirren and Dundee United. There was now a spring in the step, and a new vibrancy among the songs and chants of the fans. The stadium looked good, and players wanted to come here – and to stay.

There was definite hard luck at Motherwell one Sunday night when a ball was clearly over the line for a goal and not given by referee Hugh Dallas. That game was a 3–3 draw, but then there were good wins over Kilmarnock, St Johnstone and Hearts, the only fly in the ointment being an unlucky exit from Europe. On the other hand, progress was made in the League Cup.

But then came the inexplicable events of 26 November. In the context of the season and events both before and after, a scoreline of Rangers 5 Celtic 1 defied analysis. No real excuse was possible, and it was simply a collective bad day. Conversely, it was possibly Rangers' only good day of the season. Even more worrying was Easter Road on Wednesday night when Celtic, unable to leave Saturday's bad result behind them, struggled to a tepid and insipid 0–0 draw.

The danger signals were up, but fortunately Celtic rallied and, by the turn of the year, were so far ahead of Rangers and anyone else that bookmakers were reluctant to take bets on the League. Dunfermline were beaten convincingly, Dundee narrowly, but then Larsson scored a hat-trick as Celtic beat Aberdeen 6–0 on 16 December, then with two away wins over St Mirren and Dundee United on either side of Christmas, Celtic took over, registering another 6–0 win, this time with Larsson scoring four, over Kilmarnock on 2 January before the winter shutdown. Larsson had already scored 32 goals.

The League resumed with a win over Hearts at a snowy Tynecastle one Sunday night, and then Celtic beat Rangers twice, narrowly but decisively in both cases. The first one was in the League Cup and the second was in the League, and that basically dealt with Rangers for the season. The win in the League was 1–0 at Parkhead with a goal from Alan Thompson. Once again Fernando Ricksen did not last the 90 minutes, but this time it was referee Hugh Dallas rather than the Rangers manager who invited him to depart the scene early. Celtic's only other failure to win at this time of the season came at Easter Road on a Sunday evening, where Celtic once again showed a dismal inability to beat Hibs and had to settle for a 1–1 draw.

On a Wednesday night fixture in March at Perth (the original having been fogged off in January) Celtic beat St Johnstone 2–1 but suffered a bad blow in a broken ankle injury to Stilian Petrov, a man who had come on leaps and bounds since the arrival of O'Neill. It was a bad blow to Petrov, but such was the quality and quantity of good players at Celtic Park in those days that he was hardly missed with Lambert, Thompson, Lennon and McNamara all capable of raising their game when required. In spite of a severely depleted squad, Celtic won the League Cup on 18 March against Kilmarnock, and no prizes for guessing who scored a hat-trick!

As far as the League was concerned, it was now simply a matter of when rather than if. A hard and difficult game at Pittodrie was won 1–0 on Sunday, 1 April – the fast-running Didier Agathe scoring this time – then at Celtic Park on the Wednesday night a late goal from Johann Mjallby beat a hard-working and praiseworthy Dundee side. All this meant that the League Championship could join the League Cup if Celtic could beat St Mirren at Parkhead in the early kick-off game of Saturday, 7 April. If not, another five games remained for Celtic to complete the job!

St Mirren were facing relegation, and had so few supporters that Celtic took the unusual step of giving them only a small section of the South Front Stand, thus releasing more tickets for Celtic fans in the traditional Visitors section of the Lisbon Lions Stand. Ironically, it was one of Celtic's worst games of the season, but their 1–0 win was enough to release lavish celebration in the East End and the Celtic community.

The goal was scored just before half-time, and (in tune with the rest of the game) it was a miskick scored by Tommy Johnson. Tommy was not the best player in the world. He was a likeable Geordie, but somehow also an archetypal Celtic character whose underperforming career will be recalled with fondness by Celtic fans for this goal and also for the one he scored the previous year in the League Cup Final.

Thus the League was won for the 37th time, but it was not the end of the season. In the meaningless League fixtures, Celtic beat Rangers 3–0 at Ibrox just to emphasise the point, and then went on to complete a treble in the Hampden sunshine when they lifted the Scottish Cup by beating Hibs 3–0.

Larsson's 53 goals that season put him in the category of Jimmy McGrory and Jimmy Quinn, and that frankly says it all, but it must be emphasised that this was a superb team who delighted their supporters and earned the envy and admiration of everyone. They were strong, robust and no-nonsense in defence, skilful and productive in midfield, and up front they had Chris Sutton and, of course, the talismanic Swede. "Under O'Neill, everything seems possible" said the press, and very few people would disagree.

Scottish Cup Final		
Celtic 3 Hibs 0	Hampden	26 May
Scottish League Cup Final		
Celtic 3 Kilmarnock 0	Hampden	18 March
English Cup Final		
Liverpool 2 Arsenal 1	Cardiff	12 May
English League Cup Final		
Liverpool 1 Birmingham City 1 aet (Liverpool won 5-4 on penalties)	Cardiff	25 February
English League		
Manchester United		

CHAPTER 38

HOOPS, WE DID IT AGAIN

2001/02

Summer 2001 was one of those rare summers spent by Celtic supporters in a state of contentment blended with a feeling of eager anticipation for the new season to arrive. It had been a long time since we felt like that, but we now felt that the club, after years of underachievement and underinvestment, was definitely going in the right direction with a good manager and a board of directors who were not afraid to spend the necessary money.

Some new players did indeed arrive at the start of the season. There was, for example, Welsh International John Hartson, who had had a good career playing for teams like Arsenal and West Ham United. He cost a lot of money but with the prospect of a good run in the European Champions League, there did not seem to be any great shortage of money. Hartson was a striker, and a new defender appeared in the massive presence of Dianbobo Balde, a Guinean International who was actually born in France. He took the place of Ramon Vega who had had a good season while on loan in 2000/01 from Tottenham Hotspur but then had made the astonishing decision to turn Celtic down in favour of... Watford! "There are some things that a fella just can't understand" as the saying goes.

Season 2001/02 was probably the season in which Celtic actually played their best football under Martin O'Neill. Larsson was almost as prolific as he had been last season, but he was not the only one from whom the goals kept flowing, and it was slightly disappointing in that context to note that the Scottish League was the only competition won that year. Celtic seemed to reserve their worst performances for the Scottish League Cup semi-final in February against Rangers, and for the Scottish Cup Final at the end of the season against the same opponents.

The first foray into the new-style Champions League was also a disappointment. Their first game on 12 September had to be postponed because of the Twin Towers terrorist attack the day before and the quite genuine fears that a major world war, possibly a nuclear one, was imminent. Thank heavens, it didn't happen. Predictably, Celtic's performances were respectable at home but deplorable away from home, and they failed to qualify. They were,

"Hoops we did it again" says Henrik Larsson's T-shirt as he discusses the matter with his fellow Swede Johan Mjallby.

however, given a lifeline in the UEFA Cup where they went out tragically to Valencia on a penalty shoot-out.

The Scottish Premier League provided fewer problems. The season opened with three wins against St Johnstone at Celtic Park, Kilmarnock at Rugby Park and then Hearts at home. The games were won with a degree of ease, and the first check was at Almondvale Park, home of newly promoted Livingston whose co-managers were Jim Leishman and our old friend David Hay. Livi had already drawn at Ibrox this season, and this game gave them an Old Firm "double" when it ended 0–0, and Henrik Larsson missed a penalty kick! This was looked upon as if an earthquake had struck Almondvale, but one supporter summed it up by saying "So? He's human after all!" The following week the human Larsson got back on track, scoring as Celtic beat Hibs 4–1.

September was a good month. Dundee, a side that Celtic had often struggled against in the past, were swept aside 4–0 at Dens Park, Aberdeen were defeated at Celtic Park, and then Rangers were dealt with 2–0 at Ibrox with goals from Stilian Petrov and Alan Thompson. Dundee United's traditional "parking the team bus in the penalty area" approach to games at Parkhead came to grief as Celtic beat them 5–1 with a hat-trick from John Hartson, a goal from Bobo Balde and another from a very impressive youngster whose pants always looked too large for him. This was Shaun Maloney.

As the days shortened Celtic developed the agreeable habit of being able to score late to win games. This, naturally, frustrated the hell out of our opponents, but it was good professional stuff, showing that Celtic had a team which not only could play football but also had the "never say die" attitude which characterises champions. On 27 October, for example, at Parkhead, Kilmarnock seemed to have managed to frustrate Celtic and keep them to a 0–0 draw but had wasted so much time that the referee added on five minutes. A great cheer arose at this, and even though some of the weaker brethren of the support had given up and gone home, the remainder stayed and cheered on the team until Celtic scored a very late winner, the ball coming off what might genteelly be described as Joos Valgaeren's "abdomen".

It happened again the following week at Perth. In truth this game had been one of Celtic's poorer performances of the season, with Darren Dods of St Johnstone having accomplished the rare feat of scoring at both ends, and the game was heading to a 1–1 draw. "This is nae use", "We'll have tae improve", "What's gaun wrong?" were all heard by departing fans pursuing the warmth of their bus on a cold day. But then a free kick on the edge of the box, a lovely curler from Henrik Larsson, and they all came back singing the praises of their hero!

A Larsson penalty was enough to beat Hearts and set up a new SPL record of 10 straight wins, and then Celtic edged it over Rangers to win 2–1 at Celtic Park at the end of the month. Hibs, Dunfermline Athletic and Dundee were all then competently dispatched before Celtic lost their first and only game in the SPL that season. It was at Pittodrie in an early Saturday evening fixture a few days before

Christmas. Conditions were icy, and Aberdeen adapted better than Celtic did, winning the game by converting a penalty kick, and then taking advantage of an awful blunder by goalkeeper Rab Douglas who had not, in all honesty, had the best of nights. Some of the less well intellectually endowed of the Pittodrie support threw snowballs at the Celtic players.

This dampened the Christmas festivities, but only slightly, and in any case the mark of a good team is that they can bounce back from adversity (if it could be called that when Celtic were still so far ahead) and this Celtic did by beating Dundee United 4–0 at Tannadice before the New Year, and then taking care of Motherwell, Kilmarnock, St Johnstone, Hearts and Livingston before January was out.

Only two more points were dropped before the League was won and these were to Hibs in early February and to Rangers in March. A 4–0 win at Motherwell on Wednesday, 19 March meant that Celtic would win the League again in early April against Livingston, exactly 52 weeks after they had done so against St Mirren last year. Once more it was a Saturday lunchtime kick-off, but the difference this year lay in the fact that Celtic turned on a top-notch performance to show the worldwide TV audience just why they considered themselves to be worthy champions.

Celtic were 4–0 up at half-time with two goals each (superb ones) from both Henrik Larsson and John Hartson. In a rather boring second half, Larsson scored again to give him a hat-trick and even Livingston's goal was given a cheer by a somewhat bored Celtic crowd, who were becoming rather impatient for the final whistle and the beginning of the celebrations.

The final League table saw Celtic on 103 points, then a record for the League in the "three points for a win" era. They were 18 points ahead of second-placed Rangers. The winning of the Scottish League was a comprehensive triumph for Celtic. Once again Martin O'Neill had turned up trumps, and it was a great triumph for the insignificant-looking Irishman whose praises were sung constantly by the support.

Scottish Cup Final		
Rangers 3 Celtic 2	Hampden	4 May
Scottish League Cup Final		
Rangers 4 Ayr United 0	Hampden	17 March
English Cup Final		
Arsenal 2 Chelsea 0	Cardiff	4 May
English League Cup Final		
Blackburn Rovers 2 Tottenham Hotspur 1	Cardiff	24 February
English League		
Arsenal		

CHAPTER 39

CELTIC AT THEIR ZENITH

2003/04

Summer 2003 was a bitter-sweet time for Celtic and their supporters. On the one hand the club's European credentials had been re-established with the trip to Seville, but on the other hand, they had lost not only in Seville but in all three Scottish tournaments as well. Clearly the eye had been taken off the ball in both domestic Cups, but in the Scottish Premier League, Celtic had lost simply because they had scored fewer goals at Kilmarnock on the last Sunday than Rangers had against Dunfermline at Ibrox.

Allegations had been made by some of the Celtic support, and by Chris Sutton in particular, that Dunfermline had not put as much effort into their game at Ibrox as one felt they should. Oddly enough, it was an opinion shared by quite a few Dunfermline supporters, and it was an issue that rankled with quite a few people who claimed to have seen, for example, relatives of Dunfermline's manager enjoying Ibrox hospitality after the game.

Whatever the truth of these allegations, O'Neill and Celtic were also aware that they had themselves to blame to an extent as well. In the run-in, for example, there had been a 1–1 draw with Dundee at Dens Park, and then a 1–2 defeat from Hearts at Tynecastle – both immediately before both legs of the UEFA Cup semi-final. The lesson here was obvious. No tournament should be given any kind of precedence over any other. And the Scottish Premier League was as important as any other tournament, and possibly more so.

Ironically, Celtic's first League fixture of the 2003/04 season was at "the bed", as some supporters unkindly called East End Park, Dunfermline, in an sly reference to Dunfermline's perceived "lying down" to Rangers in May. There was certainly no "lying down" that day, but there was very little good football either and a crowd of 10,000 saw a goalless draw in the Dunfermline heat on a windless day which did nothing for the advocates of summer football. Dunfermline's excessive celebrations at the end did little to help relationships between the fans either – after all, a goalless draw at home is seldom a matter for such ecstasy! – and this was a shame, for in the past, there had always been a good atmosphere when Celtic went to East End Park.

It was not a great start, but Celtic would not now drop another point in the SPL until 14 March 2004. Twenty-five straight wins was a tremendous achievement, and they were delivered by a talented set of players grimly determined that there would not be any more heartbreaking last day losing of the League Championship. Nor were there very many of these games in which the word "lucky" could be used of Celtic. There was sometimes the very necessary "grinding out" of a win as

Henryk Larsson's mother must have forgotten to tell him that it was rude to stick out your tongue!

a team played above themselves to make life difficult for Celtic, but seldom could the press honestly claim that Celtic got all the breaks of a refereeing decision, for example.

New players were introduced in the process of this season. Stan Varga was a good defender, as indeed was John Kennedy (whose Celtic career was to be cut tragically short by a horrendous injury). Ross Wallace made an appearance, and Stephen Pearson was signed in the January transfer window from Motherwell, but possibly the best prospect was Liam Miller. This boy (sadly no longer with us, as he died of pancreatic cancer in 2018) had talent and it was believed that he would be an influential part of Celtic for many years. He certainly impressed in the games that he played before the New Year but he suddenly announced in January 2004 that he had signed a pre-contract agreement with Manchester United. He then wondered why he disappeared from the scene, as O'Neill wisely kept him out of the side! It would be a decision that Miller would bitterly regret.

In the 25-game run (a British record) Celtic beat Rangers comfortably twice. John Hartson's goal was enough to do the trick at Ibrox in early October, and the game at Parkhead on 3 January was a very one-sided affair with the 3–0 scoreline flattering Rangers. With Celtic now 11 points ahead at the halfway stage, bookmakers closed all their books on the Scottish Premier League, and even Rangers' manager Alex McLeish conceded that it would be difficult, if not impossible, to catch Celtic! And it was only halfway!

Celtic were also severe on other teams. Hibs were on the wrong end of 6–0 on 27 December (for daring to beat a slightly weakened Celtic in the League Cup nine days earlier) and Dundee United got 5–1 and 5–0 both home and away. Celtic also went "nap" over Dunfermline and Kilmarnock and a very poor Aberdeen side were lucky to get off with 4–0. It was great for the supporters to watch as players like Sutton, Larsson and Petrov simply strutted their stuff – and no one could live with them.

And all this was achieved while the team were doing reasonably well in Europe – not well enough to qualify for the final stages of the Champions League, but enough to get them to the UEFA Cup after Christmas (where they would beat Barcelona over two legs!) and seldom had there been a time in Celtic's history when the team's prestige was so high.

There was one rather large fly in the ointment, however. Henrik Larsson announced his desire to move on in the summer. It was a dignified, professional decision, so typical of the man. No amount of persuasion seemed able to make him change his mind, and although he moved on to Barcelona (winning a Champions League medal) and Manchester United, he will never be anything else than Henrik Larsson of Celtic.

On 14 March, when Livingston (in administration!) were winning the Scottish League Cup by beating Hibs 2–0 at Hampden, Motherwell earned a lucky draw at Celtic Park to end the run of victories. Hearts would also get a draw at Tynecastle three weeks later, but Rangers were disposed of yet again at Ibrox on 28 March. Larsson scored with a header, and then set up Alan Thompson for another while in the rear, young John Kennedy and emerging goalkeeper David Marshall were superb, stopping everything that the hysterical Rangers could throw at them.

But John Kennedy was badly injured playing for Scotland in a game that he would have done well to avoid, and his absence may have had something to do with Celtic's European run eventually coming to a halt against Villarreal on 14 April. Four days later, however, on Sunday, 18 April at Rugby Park (and with a whole six League fixtures remaining) Celtic clinched the League with a 1–0 win over Kilmarnock. The only goal of the game was scored by Stilian Petrov from a

Larsson pass in what was, in all honesty, not one of Celtic's better performances this season. And yet it was so appropriate to win it at Rugby Park, where they had fallen short the year before by simply failing to score enough goals on the last day. Martin O' Neill had now won three League titles out of four, each one by a clear margin and with games to spare.

Celtic eventually lost to Aberdeen at Celtic Park on the Wednesday, thus ending a 77-game unbeaten domestic run at Parkhead. It did not really matter, of course, but it was sad nevertheless. They also lost to Dunfermline on the day that the trophy was presented, but they won the two games that mattered – over Rangers and more importantly over Dunfermline in the Scottish Cup Final, as Henrik Larsson bowed out with two superb goals. A League and Cup double eased the pain as we faced the prospect of life without Henrik Larsson.

Scottish Cup Final		
Celtic 3 Dunfermline Athletic 1	Hampden	22 May
Scottish League Cup Final		
Livingston 2 Hibs 1	Hampden	14 March
English Cup Final		
Manchester United 3 Millwall 0	Cardiff	22 May
English League Cup Final		
Middlesbrough 2 Bolton Wanderers 1	Cardiff	29 February
English League		
Arsenal		

CHAPTER 40

STRACHAN TURNS UP TRUMPS

2005/06

Every Celtic supporter who was alive at the time will recall with horror the events of Black Sunday, 22 May 2005, when Scott McDonald scored the two goals in the last few minutes to take the League from Celtic. It is an urban myth, however, to suggest that Scott McDonald was the only reason for Celtic's losing the League Championship. Celtic should have scored more goals at Fir Park that day, but in any case there had been a loss of form in the run in to the end of the season, which included, for example, losing to both Hearts and Hibs at Celtic Park.

Martin O'Neill's mind was clearly elsewhere, concerned about serious domestic issues, and he departed the club soon after Black Sunday, although he did leave one final gift in the shape of the Scottish Cup. Martin left with happy memories and best wishes. The choice of successor, however, raised more than a few eyebrows.

The mantle fell upon Gordon Strachan. Strachan had been a great player for Aberdeen and Scotland, but his past record as a manager did not impress too much. His spells at Coventry and Southampton had been nothing to write home about, but there were stronger reservations about him than that. Basically, Celtic supporters did not like him. While with Aberdeen, he had played a large part in the sending off of Roy Aitken in the 1984 Cup Final and he had been attacked

Triumphant scenes after the title was won in April 2006.

physically at least twice on the field by maverick Celtic supporters. While no one can condone such violent behaviour, it could not be disputed that Strachan had brought it on himself to a certain extent by his gestures, his faking and exaggeration of injuries and general stirring of the public. In addition, when interviewed on TV, he was often unnecessarily cheeky and impudent in his answers to polite, bland, harmless questions.

He did not seem to be a good choice, and that impression gained ground when, in his first game, Celtic went to Artmedia Bratislava, hardly one of the giants of Europe, and the team of bewildered, disorientated players lost 0–5. In the first SPL game, the team drew 4–4 at Motherwell, a game which delighted the TV neutrals because it certainly had a high entertainment level, but the Celtic defending was woeful. Already a "Strachan must go" campaign was beginning to form, and there is little doubt that, had the Artmedia game not been his very first game, he would have had to pay the price that John Barnes did in 2000 for Inverness Caledonian Thistle or that Tony Mowbray would do in 2010 for St Mirren.

But these were early days, and wisely the board backed him as he and Celtic "dug in". Steve McManus slowly began to stabilise things at the back, Shaun Maloney was given a much deserved run in the team, and three foreign players came in, all of whom would be significant. There was goalkeeper Artur Boruc, an occasionally controversial character from Poland, a fellow compatriot of his by the name of Maciej Zurawski who, in spite of his languid uninterested look, proved to be a good goalscorer, and then Celtic's first ever Japanese player in the shape of Shunsuke Nakamura, a man of dazzling ability with a particular and welcome knack of scoring free kicks.

The early exit from Europe, painful as it was at the time, was possibly a blessing in disguise in that it allowed the new Celtic team, now of course shorn of Henrik Larsson, to develop. By Christmas the development was in full swing. They had lost to Rangers in August, but had compensated for that by beating them twice handsomely at Celtic Park in successive matches in November, one in the League and one in the League Cup, and their only other defeat before the New Year had been a funny one to Dunfermline Athletic at the end of November, a defeat only partially to be explained by the absence of Maloney and Nakamura.

A feature of the season so far had been the undeniable fact that Celtic's main challengers had been not Rangers, but Hearts. Indeed, much attention had been focussed on Tynecastle where the Lithuanian owner who had informed the gullible that Hearts were going to win the Champions League, kept grabbing the headlines by doing eccentric things like sacking manager George Burley on a Saturday morning before a game! They did, however, have some good players, a now mobilised and active support and were always a challenge, even though over the course of that season, they had four managers!

Celtic however were now four points ahead in the SPL when they went to Tynecastle on New Year's Day. It turned out to be the decisive day of the League race, and was one of the best games ever seen between these two teams. Hearts were two goals up and in command, but then Stephen Pearson, somewhat of an underperformer hitherto, came on as a substitute, scored almost immediately from a Shaun Maloney cross and then took control of the game as Celtic fought back to equalise through McManus within the last five minutes, and then the same player scored the winner in injury time!

Celtic were now comfortable at the top of the League, but then came an inexplicable Scottish Cup loss to Clyde at Broadwood. Strachan made a gross error in giving a Celtic debut to two players on the same day. One was Roy Keane, who was now fulfilling a boyhood ambition of playing for Celtic but was now clearly past his best, and the other was a Chinaman called Du Wei who, after this game, more or less disappeared and was never heard of again. In addition, the other players took Clyde far too lightly and paid the penalty.

Once again there were mutterings about Strachan as he tried unconvincingly to laugh it off, but what no one could argue about was the League form, which continued to be very good indeed, including a psychologically vital 1–0 defeat of Rangers at Ibrox in February, followed by an SPL record 8–1 hammering of Dunfermline at East End Park which included the rare sight of Neil Lennon scoring a goal. The only slight blot was a 3–3 draw with Dundee United at Celtic Park, and the team was also making progress in the Scottish League Cup which they duly won on 19 March, something that did a great deal to compensate for there being no Scottish Cup this year.

Also in March, good wins over Aberdeen, Hibs, Inverness and Livingston meant that the SPL, which had for long been a formality, could be clinched on Wednesday, 5 April when Hearts came to Celtic Park. A packed Parkhead saw a tough encounter but a fine strike from John Hartson – who was celebrating his 31st birthday that night – in the early stages was enough to put Celtic ahead. Then came a vigorous fightback from Hearts – enough to show any doubting Parkhead

Scottish Cup Final		
Hearts 1 Gretna 1 aet	Hampden	13 May
(Hearts won 4-2 on penalties)		
Scottish League Cup Final		
Celtic 3 Dunfermline Athletic 0	Hampden	19 March
English Cup Final		
Liverpool 3 West Ham United 3	Cardiff	13 May
(Liverpool won 3-1 on penalties)		
English League Cup Final		
Manchester United 4 Wigan Athletic 0	Cardiff	26 February
English League		
Chelsea		

Thomas that under more stable leadership, it might have been a different story – but Artur Boruc and the centre-half pairing of Bobo Balde and Stephen McManus were at their best that night, and the full-time whistle came to a tremendous cheer and outburst of applause for the champions.

One had to give a great deal of credit to Gordon Strachan, a man who had had to overcome a certain amount of hostility and prejudice against him at the start of the season but who had overcome it splendidly and was now accepted as one of us, albeit with a little reluctance from some. He had bought well, and had moulded together a good side which had now won the Scottish League Championship for the 40th time.

The rest of the season fizzled out with the highlight being a goalless draw against Rangers at Parkhead, and the lowlight a 0–3 drubbing at Tynecastle, something that gave the Jambos something to cheer about. They would be even happier at the Scottish Cup Final when they beat (albeit on a penalty shoot-out) Gretna (yes, Gretna!) in one of the more remarkable stories of the early years of the 21st century.

CHAPTER 41

NAKA'S RISING SUN

2006/07

This was a curious season. The SPL was won (very comfortably) and so was the Scottish Cup, but the standard of play seldom reached any great heights. A certain amount of success was achieved in Europe with three good home wins over Benfica, Copenhagen and Manchester United and genuine hard luck against AC Milan, but this season saw very little challenge in Scotland with the laughable spectacle of Rangers having been bullied by the media into appointing Paul le Guen as manager. The poor man was unable to cope with Scotland, fielding players who were, frankly, not Rangers class, being pushed around by some of the senior players and struggling even to speak the English language. It was very tragic for Monsieur le Guen who was a success elsewhere, but was not the first or last to discover what a strange place Scotland (and Ibrox in particular) is.

Strachan brought a European dimension to Celtic this season, and this was to a certain extent reflected in the signings – Jiri Jarosik, Evander Sno, Thomas Gravesen and the impressively named Jan Vennegoor of Hesselink. Not all of them starred for Celtic – in fact one or two of them can justifiably claim that they were underused by Strachan – and there were also a trio of Scotsmen who joined the club – Gary Caldwell and Derek Riordan from Hibs, and (controversially) Kenny Miller, one-time of Rangers. The January window would bring another ex-Rangers player in Steven Pressley, and Paul Hartley who always claimed to be a Celtic supporter but had never been anything other than a doughty opponent when playing for Hearts, an organisation which was now beginning to show signs of serious disintegration, even though they did register a win over Celtic in the second game of the year.

Other than that, though, League form was steady until the turn of the season. September saw a competent 1–0 win at Pittodrie, a very satisfying 2–0 defeat of Rangers at Celtic Park with Kenny Miller scoring one of his best goals, and then there was a somewhat remarkable 2–1 win over Hearts at Celtic Park in early November. Hearts were 1–0 up and looking comfortable until Jiri Jarosik scored with a header to give Celtic what looked like an honourable draw, but then in extra-time, Craig Gordon, still playing for Hearts, allowed a McManus shot to squirm through his hands and into the net to give Celtic a sweet, but not necessarily totally deserved, victory.

Falkirk would turn out to be a difficult team for Celtic this year. They put Celtic out of the League Cup (on penalties) after a dreadful Celtic performance in the 90 minutes and extra-time, and twice in the League before Christmas Celtic had to dig deep to beat the Bairns 1–0 after Falkirk had outplayed Celtic

Shunsuke Nakamura with his hair all over the place at Dunfermline.

for large stretches of the game. It was that kind of a season for Celtic – 1–0 and 2–1 being frequent scorelines with the opposition able to claim that they had enough of the play, but Celtic were often professional enough (our opponents called it "lucky") to win through in the end, often with late goals.

Boxing Day at Parkhead, for example, saw Dundee United two up but Celtic came back through Darren O'Dea and Nakamura to earn a 2–2 draw. O'Dea was on as substitute after Bobo Balde had been taken off with a broken leg from which his career did not really recover. Fir Park the day before Hogmanay saw the boot on the other foot, however. This time it was Motherwell who equalised well into injury time after Derek Riordan had put Celtic ahead. Gordon Strachan was seen by the TV cameras to vent his frustration by kicking a water bottle, but was honest and gracious enough later on to admit that Celtic were poor. Yet they were way ahead in the League race, so much so, that the League was already being conceded in certain quarters.

Another seven victories (most of them in the same mould) followed in the New Year – the game at Tynecastle on 14 January being characterised by a great match-winning goal from Jiri Jarosik – although the game at Pittodrie was far more convincing than the 2–1 scoreline would have suggested and the feeling was growing that this style, however lacking flair and out of touch with the Celtic tradition, was possibly what was required for European football.

Sadly, no, but the exit to AC Milan was a genuinely good performance and it might have been all different if the exhausted Nakamura had still been on the field when Celtic were awarded a late free kick, but what was a great deal more concerning was the almost immediate loss of form in the SPL. The 0–1 loss to Rangers at Parkhead the following Sunday was narrow and Celtic probably deserved a draw in spite of some players looking out of touch, but then the following week, Falkirk who had lost their previous eight games, suddenly discovered their form and beat Celtic 1–0. Once again Celtic looked disjointed, Craig Beattie missed a penalty and rumours began to emerge about some players finding it difficult to live with Gordon Strachan, who did indeed do little to help his cause, as his team selections were sometimes strange.

The apologetic limp towards the League title continued with a 1–1 draw at Tannadice Park. Nakamura had scored a free kick but the forwards could not add any more, and the penalty was paid when Dundee United scored a late equaliser. The rot was stopped, in a way, when Celtic at last recorded a win. This came when Motherwell arrived at Celtic Park, and Derek Riordan in one of his rare starts for the club scored the only goal of the game. This win and results elsewhere meant that Celtic were now only three points away from the title, which could therefore be clinched at Kilmarnock on 22 April if Celtic could win that game.

It was a rare treat for Kilmarnock to see so many fans in their ground and maximum exposure from the radio and TV companies. The weather was good as well, and Kilmarnock opened both the end stands for Celtic supporters – a wise decision which earned them a lot of money and looking round at the meagre home support, one wonders why they didn't open the whole ground for the green and white brigade who had descended on Ayrshire in large numbers. Those who didn't have tickets went instead to a local pub, when they could well have filled some of the empty seats in the Main Stand.

Celtic had the bonus of the return of defender John Kennedy some three years after his horrendous injury. They were 1–0 up at half-time, a fine glancing header from Vennegoor of Hesselink from a Nakamura corner kick, but then complacency crept in again in the shape of failing to bury the game and allowing Colin Nish to equalise for the home side. It looked as if it were going to be a draw and that Celtic would have to finish the job in one of their remaining four fixtures, but then in the 92nd minute, Nakamura was clumsily pushed in the back by a Kilmarnock defender just in "Nakamura territory" outside the penalty area.

It was as if the script had been written, for the lovely wee Japanese artist curled the ball in at the far post with the added bonus of making the ball hit the ground almost as it was crossing the line, something that made it even more difficult for the goalkeeper to stop the ball. Joy was unconfined among the Celtic fans worldwide including one or two newly formed Celtic supporters clubs in Japan, where it was now possible to watch Celtic games. Nakamura had been the star of the Celtic team all season and it was only fitting that he should be feted in this way!

The remaining four irrelevant games of the season were awful. A win over Hibs, but defeats to Aberdeen, Hearts and Rangers, but the season finished on another high note when we beat Dunfermline Athletic in the Scottish Cup Final. Somewhat fittingly for the season, it was a pedestrian (to put it tactfully) Cup Final but eventually the unlikely figure of Jean Joel Perrier Doumbe, the full-back from the Cameroons, scored a fairly scrappy goal and gave Celtic a Double.

Scottish Cup Final		
Celtic 1 Dunfermline Athletic 0	Hampden	26 May
Scottish League Cup Final		
Hibs 5 Kilmarnock 1	Hampden	18 March
English Cup Final		
Chelsea 1 Manchester United 0	Wembley	19 May
English League Cup Final		
Chelsea 2 Arsenal 1	Cardiff	25 February
English League		
Manchester United		

CHAPTER 42

BACK FROM THE DEAD

2007/08

This was in some ways Celtic's most remarkable League-winning season of them all. In early April they seemed down and out with not a hope of any kind of resurrection, and yet with a combination of results, and a grim determination to do well combined with a little good fortune, by 22 May on a Thursday night at Tannadice Park, Gordon Strachan had led Celtic to become champions for the third year in a row.

It was not a good season. Europe was once again creditable and the eventual bowing of the knee to Barcelona was hardly a major disgrace. The exits from the two Scottish domestic tournaments, however, were a little disappointing – to Hearts in the Scottish League Cup, and to Aberdeen in the Scottish Cup, the Scottish Cup being all the more heartbreaking because it was a replay and Celtic had seemed to have done the hard work at Pittodrie in the first game.

These disappointments were all the harder to take because it was a season that Rangers were doing well in all their tournaments. They in fact won both the Scottish League Cup and Scottish Cup that year and reached the final of the UEFA Cup. We know now that history would prove that it was all done by dodgy deals, but Rangers were no insignificant outfit in 2008.

Another example of the transient nature of the crazy world of Scottish football was provided by Gretna. They had risen from nowhere to reach the Scottish Cup Final of 2006 and now they were in the SPL. The SPL who had at one point compelled Inverness to play all their home games in Aberdeen now made Gretna play all their

Gordon Strachan is not pleased with something.

games at Motherwell and sometimes Livingston. You simply could not have made all that up! Gretna FC was all based in the financial fortunes of one man, however, and it all came crashing down – but a similar thing was fated to happen to Rangers as well.

Celtic had started the League season well, beating Hearts and Aberdeen for example, but had fallen at Easter Road thanks to a last-minute goalkeeping error from Artur Boruc, who could on occasion be guilty of such things. Nevertheless, they arrived at Ibrox top of the League with new signings generally doing well – Maximo Donati had scored a late and decisive goal at Pittodrie, Scott McDonald from Motherwell was among the goals, and Scott Brown from Hibs, though a little hot-headed from time to time, was showing signs of developing into a really good and creative midfielder.

The visit to Ibrox on 20 October, however, brought things to a shuddering halt with a 0–3 defeat. There was a ready-made excuse in some of the decisions of Mike McCurry – the "sinister minister" of a Christian church. He would eventually be removed from the referees' list after a sexual scandal – but the truth of that matter was that Celtic played very badly that day, and at least some of the nine bookings of Celtic players were justified.

Strachan was saved by the qualification for the last 16 of the Champions' League, but December saw another dip with a defeat at Inverness, and two home games against St Mirren and Hibs where they could do no more than draw. The tragic death of Phil O'Donnell on the field on 29 December (Celtic had beaten Gretna 3–0 that day) meant that the games against Rangers and Motherwell had to be postponed.

There were two significant signings in January in Barry Robson and Georgios Samaras (Robson scored with his first kick for the club at Aberdeen!) and Aiden McGeady was beginning now to live up to his early promise, as the team kept winning its League games, even though it was doing less well in other tournaments. But the danger signals came up again with a feckless 0–0 draw against Dundee United one Wednesday night in March at Parkhead, and when Rangers beat us 1–0 at Ibrox in a dreadful game at the end of the month, making them six points ahead with a game in hand, that, frankly, seemed to be that. Things took a decided turn for the worse a week later in early April, when we went down 0–1 to ten-man Motherwell at an angry Parkhead, and the League was now generally believed to be a thing of fantasy for this season, even though Rangers themselves could only draw that weekend.

An incurable optimist said, however, that Celtic still had to play Rangers twice at Celtic Park. If Celtic could win these two, if Celtic could win the rest of their games and if Rangers could draw twice with other teams, then Celtic could do it yet! It was an absurd scenario. Maybe Celtic could beat Rangers twice, maybe Rangers could draw twice, but could Celtic hope to win all their games to come – two trips to Motherwell, one to Dundee United, and then Aberdeen and Hibs at home? No! Impossible! Yet, incredibly, it happened.

A factor that entered the equation was Rangers fixtures. They were still in Europe and in the Scottish Cup as well, and (as Celtic themselves have discovered too often in the past), when that happens, the eye does get taken off the ball. Celtic's goal difference was better as well, and it would become more so. Another factor was the pitch at Fir Park where Celtic had to play twice and Rangers once. Frankly it was a disgrace, the situation not helped by being played on far too often (Gretna had played their homes games there as well) and even the TV commentators were heard to use phrases like "tattie field" about it, and to make sarcastic comments about whether the Motherwell groundsman should enter for the Groundsman of the Year competition and so on.

Be that as it may, Celtic had first use of the tattie field, and without playing in any way well, nevertheless beat Motherwell 4–1 on 13 April, when Rangers were involved in Scottish Cup business. Then on the following midweek, the first of the two Parkhead fixtures against Rangers was played, and Celtic won 2–1 in a remarkable game which saw a lovely Nakamura goal, Scott McDonald miss a penalty and Jan Vennegoor of Hesselink score a late injury time winner with his head. While it was lovely to see detestable people like Barry Ferguson and Nacho Novo get their comeuppance, we were all, however, uncomfortably aware that Rangers still held the whip hand.

Rangers were still involved on Scottish Cup business the following Saturday, but Celtic played and beat Aberdeen 1–0 in a distinctly unconvincing performance. The goal scored by Georgios Samaras, however, meant that Celtic were now top of the League, although Rangers had two games in hand. Next midweek saw Rangers involved in Europe. It might have been better for them if they had lost, but they won through. They did not win at Celtic Park, however, when they came again on Sunday, 27 April.

Celtic's 3–2 victory (two Scott McDonald goals and a Barry Robson penalty) meant that Celtic were now five points ahead but Rangers had three games in hand, and could still win the League by four points. But this game was significant for several reasons. One was that it showed the world that Celtic were the better side, another was that it brought a spring in the step to Celtic players and supporters, and the third was that the pressure now began to mount on Rangers.

Saturday, 3 May saw Celtic come from behind to beat Motherwell on that dreadful pitch, and then on Sunday, 4 May, a crack was heard, coming from Easter Road as Hibs heroically held out to defy Rangers and gain a 0–0 draw. But Celtic were now seven points ahead and Rangers still had three games in hand. Annoyingly, they won one of them when they beat Motherwell 1–0 at Ibrox in midweek. Celtic were now four points ahead with two games to play, but Rangers had four games left.

The sunny weekend of 10/11 May saw both teams win, with Rangers beating Dundee United controversially at Ibrox (Dundee United were denied a blatant penalty and had a legitimate goal chalked off by referee Mike McCurry) but Celtic replying with a good 2–0 win over Hibs. The following midweek was reserved for Rangers' UEFA Cup Final against Zenit St Petersburg in Manchester. They lost and their fans rioted badly.

The following day Tommy Burns died. To their eternal credit, Walter Smith, Ally McCoist and some others from Rangers FC turned up at the funeral in a Roman Catholic church a few days later, but, by this time, Celtic had gained the initiative in the League race. On Saturday, 17 May, Rangers, still struggling to cope with their defeat in Manchester and the worldwide condemnation of their fans' behaviour, travelled to play on the awful pitch of Motherwell, and could only draw. Celtic fans watched this tense game on their TVs, but full-time brought the realisation that Celtic were ahead on goal difference, even if Rangers beat St Mirren on Monday, as they duly did.

The SPL and Setanta TV had decided that both final games were to go ahead at the same time on Thursday, 22 May. Celtic went to Tannadice knowing that they would be okay as long as they won and Rangers did not hammer Aberdeen at Pittodrie by some improbable score. 0–0 at half-time in both games, but who can forget the animation among the Celtic infiltrators in the Dundee United stand spotted on TV telling us that Aberdeen had scored? Immediately after that, Paul Hartley took a corner in front of the Shed, and Jan Vennegoor of Hesselink rose like a bird to head home. It was a memorable night, and a memorable finish to a scarcely believable campaign.

Scottish Cup Final		
Rangers 3 Queen of the South 2	Hampden	24 May
Scottish League Cup Final		
Rangers 2 Dundee United 2	Hampden	16 March
(Rangers won 3-2 on penalties)		
English Cup Final		
Portsmouth 1 Cardiff City 0	Wembley	17 May
English League Cup Final		
Tottenham Hotspur 2 Chelsea 1 aet	Wembley	24 February
English League		
Manchester United		

CHAPTER 43

"WE'RE HAVING A PARTY..."

2011/12

The defining moment of this season came on St Valentine's Day, 14 February, when Rangers went into administration. The news of Rangers going bust had been brewing for some considerable time and in some ways it was a shock to realise that all the prophecies in song about "The Huns are going bust" and "We're having a party when Rangers die" had indeed come true.

While one could have a certain amount of pity for some of their supporters – the decent kind (of whom there are many) – it was not easy to feel anything other than a sense of justice that Nemesis had at last caught up with "you who have harried and held... and you who have bullied and bribed" as the Irish patriot put it. Their dodgy deals, their illegal payments to players, their refusal to pay Income Tax, their policy of religious discrimination, the thuggery of their support had now been paid back with interest. Justice had prevailed.

Nor could one readily sympathise with the singers of sectarian songs, in particular the grossly offensive one about the famine being over or those who as recently as 2008 had fouled Scotland's name in Manchester and elsewhere. It was extremely ironic that those who sang the praises so heartily of Her Majesty the Queen were lovers of a club who failed to pay any revenue to Her Majesty's Revenue Commission!

So where did all this leave Celtic? One myth that has already found its way onto one or two revisionist websites is that the points deduction imposed on Rangers for financial maladministration meant that Celtic would now win the League. This is incorrect. Celtic, having had a poor autumn both in Scotland and in Europe, had in fact rallied and by 28 December, when Joe Ledley headed Celtic to a 1–0 victory on a windy night at Celtic Park, Celtic had gone in front and stayed in front.

The calendar year of 2011 had not been a good one. Only the Scottish Cup triumph over Motherwell had made life worth living, after Celtic had unaccountably blown up in Inverness and then a nana at Tynecastle had attacked Neil Lennon – an event which was disturbingly cheered by some of the Hearts supporters – and

The strips are horrible but Glenn Loovens, Ki Sung Yueng, Anthony Stokes and Beram Kayal are happy after a goal at Kilmarnock.

then when the 2011/12 season started Celtic, admittedly hampered by a bad injury sustained at Pittodrie in Aberdeen to the hitherto very effective Emilio Izaguirre, had lost to Rangers, Hearts and St Johnstone as well as flopping disastrously to Sion of Switzerland in Europe. Yet Celtic were allowed back in to the UEFA Cup because Sion had fielded an illegal player. It would have been better if they hadn't, because the games against Udinese, Atletico Madrid and Rennes were uninspiring, to put it mildly.

At one point the team were 18 points behind Rangers, but they had pulled it back. A turning point of sorts may have been at Kilmarnock on 15 October, more precisely at half-time in this game. Celtic were 0–3 down, and Neil Lennon is on record as saying that he thought he was facing the boot. That might have been true, but Celtic rallied in the second half to earn a 3–3 draw although, late in the game, both teams might have won the game but were betrayed by woeful finishing. It did, however, give Lennon some breathing space and slowly the team began to improve. In fact, as far as the League was concerned, they never really looked back.

The "January transfer window" was to a large extent bypassed, Celtic by choice and Rangers by necessity for they simply did not have the money, and then in early February, Rangers exited the Scottish Cup to their old Scottish Cup bogey team Dundee United. A good Scottish Cup run might have given them some encouragement and a chance to get some money together – but it would never have been enough to stave off the impatient taxman, for things had gone too far for all that.

Celtic in the meantime went from strength to strength as far as the SPL was concerned. The defence was visibly tightened with the versatile Charlie Mulgrew and Kelvin Wilson beginning to get things together, and upfront more goals began to flow from the boots of Gary Hooper, Anthony Stokes and the ever-unreliable but always wholehearted and loveable Georgios Samaras.

Yet one could never have said that this was a great Celtic team. A strong Rangers, or even a good Aberdeen or Hearts might have given them a great deal of bother, but the challenge was definitely not there this season and Celtic moved ever closer to the title.

Successive Sundays in March brought disappointments. The Scottish League Cup Final was lost in a rather supine fashion. After a great deal of competent yet lacklustre play from Celtic, Kilmarnock scored late in the game and held out against a desperate Celtic onslaught in which Celtic might just have won a penalty kick in injury time. It was a rare moment of triumph for Kilmarnock whose paltry support have had little to cheer about over the years, and even then it was marred by the death virtually on the full-time whistle of the father of one of their players, Liam Kelly.

Then Celtic could have won the Scottish League the following week, but went down to Rangers at Ibrox in a game that gave Rangers fans a little self-respect even though they had a little help from the referee who sent off two Celtic players, one of them the inoffensive Cha Du Ri and the other the very effective Victor Wanyama. Celtic's manager Neil Lennon was sent to the stand, but was advised to watch the game from the media room for his safety could not be guaranteed! It was at that point, one feels, that many more people came to the conclusion that the demise of Rangers was no real loss to the world. It was, however, a poor performance by Celtic.

But Celtic then beat St Johnstone in midweek and the League was eventually won at Kilmarnock on 7 April, a sunny lunchtime kick-off. It was the third time that Celtic had won the SPL at Rugby Park this century, but this time the game was little other than a carnival with a Celtic team showing a great deal of appetite for the ball and scoring six superb goals to raise the fairly obvious question of how on earth Kilmarnock had managed to win the Scottish League Cup Final three weeks ago.

Kilmarnock had bowed to realism and allowed Celtic fans to populate three quarters of the ground. The result was that they attracted a good crowd of 15,926 fans, and one wondered why they did not do this every time Celtic came to town. Their own fans had only the Main Stand, and even there one or two fans were seen to rise and applaud the Celtic goals. Celtic were playing in their odd "yellow with a few black stripes" strip and turned on their best performance of the season. Charlie Mulgrew scored first with a header from a Ki corner, then he himself crossed for the much despised Glenn Loovens to score with a marvellous header. Mulgrew then scored again with a lovely curling ball from the edge of the box, and half-time was reached with Celtic 4–0 up, Gary Hooper having volleyed home another one. The second half was, frankly, a bit of a bore and an anticlimax, although Celtic did manage to score another two goals through Ledley and Hooper.

So Celtic won their 43rd League Championship. It was by no means a vintage season, but the SPL Championship, absent since 2008, was a welcome returner to Celtic Park. Celtic were less successful in the Scottish Cup when they went down to Hearts in the semi-final at Hampden in a game that was decided by a very soft penalty which was a penalty only in the eyes of the referee.

Scottish Cup Final		
Hearts 5 Hibs 1	Hampden	19 May
Scottish League Cup Final		
Kilmarnock 1 Celtic 0	Hampden	18 March
English Cup Final		
Chelsea 2 Liverpool 1	Wembley	5 May
English League Cup Final		
Liverpool 2 Cardiff 2 aet (Liverpool won 3-2 on penalties)	Wembley	26 February
English League		
Manchester City		

CHAPTER 44

"AND THE CRY WAS NO MORE RANGERS"

2012/13

On 16 July 2012 the historic and totally amazing decision was reached at the AGM of the Scottish Premier League. Rangers were voted out. If someone had predicted this 10 or even five years earlier he would have been smiled at pityingly, while someone else might tactfully have suggested a visit to the doctor. Rangers, founder members of the Scottish League in 1890 and the club who had done so much to create the independent monstrosity of the Scottish Premier League at the turn of the 21st century, were now no longer a part of it, while the two Highlanders, Inverness Caledonian Thistle and Ross County, were. Dundee were invited to take Rangers place. What sort of a crazy Mad Hatter sort of world were we living in?

Conventional wisdom had always suggested that there would an "old pals network" which would have created a movement spearheaded by Celtic to save and retain Rangers. After all, it made financial sense to do so. In 2000 the Leagues had been rearranged to save Aberdeen from dropping down, and Rangers themselves had not been slow to show support for Celtic in 1952 when silly politicians and administrators were wanting them banned for displaying an Irish flag.

Kris Commons (not in picture) scores Celtic's first League goal of the season against Aberdeen at Celtic Park.

But this was a different situation. Rangers had antagonised so many clubs – Motherwell, Dundee United, Hibs, Aberdeen, for example, that everyone turned on them. Celtic tended to retain a dignified silence. But Rangers had alienated themselves by their inability or refusal to pay bills, their arrogant attitude to ticket distribution and by the boorishness of their supporters who regularly committed acts of violence on innocent Scottish towns and sang ludicrous songs about the religious wars of the past. Scotland as a nation had moved on, and there was still a sense of shame about what had happened in Manchester in 2008.

There was thus no Rangers, as Celtic began the League campaign of 2012/13. It did not take any kind of a genius to work out that Celtic were the favourites to win the Scottish Premier League. Celtic's cause was further helped by Hibs, Hearts and Aberdeen all having indifferent seasons, and the only club to put up anything approaching resistance to Celtic was Motherwell. Even then, the Fir Park men finished 16 points behind as the League was wrapped up against Inverness Caledonian Thistle on 21 April with four games to go.

It was, however, a far from vintage League campaign from Celtic. They lost seven games and finished with 79 points out of a possible 114. It is true to say that they would not have got away with that if there had been a strong Rangers or Aberdeen around, and when Englishmen made sneering remarks like "on the island of the blind, the one-eyed man is king", one had to nod in reluctant agreement.

Yet this is hard on the team as well. They also won the Scottish Cup, reached the semi-final of the Scottish League Cup and qualified for the last 16 of the European Champions League (beating Barcelona, Lionel Messi and all, in the process). But the Scottish Premier League this particular season was by no means one of the most thrilling or demanding.

The League season opened at Celtic Park with a 1–0 win over Aberdeen, the goal coming from Kris Commons who was arguably Celtic's best player at the moment. There was then a draw at Ross County, another draw when Hibs came calling, and then Celtic managed to embarrass themselves by losing pitifully to St Johnstone. McDiarmid Park (and Muirton before it) had in the past been difficult grounds for Celtic, but not in recent years and this was a particularly lacklustre and half-hearted performance from Celtic whose new foreign recruits were showing serious problems as they tried to adapt to the Scottish game.

On 27 October something historic happened. Kilmarnock, a club who had had a fair amount of success in Scottish football particularly in the 1960s, had nevertheless not beaten Celtic at Parkhead since December 1955. They brought this to an end today, and were well worth their win over a woeful Celtic side who, frankly, failed to function. Two stuttering draws against Dundee United and St Johnstone followed and there was a further defeat in November to Inverness at home.

This was really most un-Celtic form, but it was mitigated by several factors. One was that there was in all this an element of "taking the eye off the ball" with a view to doing well in Europe, another was that they still were top of the League as no single challenger had really emerged, and another was that Celtic and their supporters were celebrating on 6 November the 125th year since the legendary founding of the club at St Mary's Hall.

Form improved in December with five wins in a row, including fine performances at Tynecastle and Rugby Park which showed the television audience that this Celtic team could play good football, but the year 2012 finished with a narrow defeat to Hibs at Easter Road. Once again, this potential disaster was mitigated into only a temporary disappointment with the failure of any other team to capitalise on Celtic's off day.

But then in January, Celtic embarked on the run that would effectively win them the Scottish League. Motherwell, Hearts, Kilmarnock, Inverness and Dundee United again were all put to the sword, and even though there were further reverses including a horror show at Ross County, there was never any great doubt that the League title was coming to Celtic for the second year in a row.

Yet there was a certain amount of discontent among the supporters, mainly about the central defence and the attack. Kelvin Wilson and Efe Ambrose tended to have too many off days – in the case of the likeable Efe, rather too many spectacularly bad ones – and Gary Hooper did not seem to score as many goals as we felt that he should. Nineteen League goals were not really enough. The same could be said about Anthony Stokes. And no one divided the opinions of supporters more than Georgios Samaras. Those of us who recalled the career of John Hughes in the 1960s could see a similarity. There were some great goals – one in particular at Rugby Park, Kilmarnock in September 2008 springs to mind – but there were other times when he was frustratingly clumsy and found it hard to get going.

On the other hand, there were some really good players – Kris Commons, Joe Ledley and Charlie Mulgrew retained their popularity, while the best player was probably Viktor Wanyama - "the Kenyan Fenian" as some of the support dubbed him. In goal, Fraser Forster was totally dependable.

The most exciting game of the season was when Craig Brown's Aberdeen came to Parkhead in mid-March and Celtic fought back from being behind to win 4–3. There followed a draw at League Cup winners St Mirren, then a win over Hibs at Celtic Park. Celtic were already in the Scottish Cup Final when the League was clinched at a full Parkhead on 21 April. Symbolically, it was a dull day in the first half, but then when the sun came through in the second half, the goals began to flow – two from Gary Hooper, one from Joe Ledley and a brilliant individual goal from "gorgeous Georgios" Samaras himself as Celtic romped to a 4–1 victory.

Those who felt that the world of officialdom is 100% against Celtic had a point, one felt, when Neil Lennon was compelled to wait for 15 minutes before being allowed to talk to the Celtic crowd at the end. Neil had been banned from the touchline for criticising officials, but this particular piece of petty-mindedness seemed to lack any explanation other than sheer spite. But we waited and Neil gave his address.

The Double was completed when the Scottish Cup was won in May. The Scottish Cup Final was on a Sunday, Celtic played the game in black, and there were no Rangers. Just what on earth had happened to Scottish football? And in England who could have predicted that the two Cups would be won by Wigan and Swansea? Strange times, indeed.

Scottish Cup Final		
Celtic 3 Hibernian 0	Hampden	26 May
Scottish League Cup Final		
St Mirren 3 Hearts 2	Hampden	17 March
English Cup Final		
Wigan 1 Manchester City 0	Wembley	11 May
English League Cup Final		
Swansea 5 Bradford City 0	Wembley	24 February
English League		
Manchester United		

CHAPTER 45

WINNING AT A CANTER

2013/14

Season 2013/14 was a strange one. Once again, there was no Rangers and once again the Scottish League was won easily. But if Celtic had it easy in the Scottish League, it was more than compensated for in Europe where their Group Stage section contained AC Milan, Barcelona and Ajax – a remarkable and unusual section in that each of the four of them had won the European Cup! Celtic were, frankly, outclassed. There was one creditable win over Ajax, and a reasonable performance against Barcelona at Celtic Park, but the other games were embarrassing. And yet, there had been one night early in the season that showed Parkhead at its best. This was when Celtic qualified for the Champions League with a late James Forrest goal over Shakhtar Karagandy.

The two domestic cups were also disappointing with sub-standard performances at home to Aberdeen and (incredibly) to Morton meant that there were no Cup Final days out at – well, in fact it would have been Celtic Park, for Hampden was being readied for the Commonwealth games. Celtic won the Scottish League by a country mile, and it is still rather difficult to explain why Neil Lennon chose to resign at the end of the season. Or was he pushed? Was it all too easy for him? Did he want a challenge? Did he want more money to finance a challenge on Europe? No really satisfactory explanation has as yet appeared.

The League season was remarkable for the long run without losing a goal. From 23 November until 25 February the team did not lose a single goal in the Scottish League. For a club that traditionally over the years has been criticised by its own supporters for

Neil Lennon.

having a "leaky defence" – a criticism when went back to the days of Billy McNeill and beyond – this was quite a feat. Thirteen League games without a goal conceded beat the record set by the mighty Shaw, McNair and Dodds of exactly 100 years before, and full credit must be paid to men like Fraser Forster, Emilio Izaguirre, Virgil Van Dijk and even the much-maligned Efe Ambrose for the part they played in establishing this record. Goals were conceded in other competitions during this run but not in the Scottish League. If a team can go that length of time without conceding a goal (the 100% record ran for 15 games), they must be a good step or two along the road to winning the League.

But there were deficiencies in other areas of the side. Although the midfield tended to win most battles and the defence was solid, there was always the feeling that not enough goals were being scored. Four out of the five games, for example, between 14 December and New Year's Day were 1–0 victories, and the attendances began to reflect the poor fare on offer. "Competence" was the word used rather than anything to do with exhilarating entertainment.

There was only one defeat in the League – to Aberdeen at Pittodrie on the night of 25 February that the long unbeaten run was broken. Even then, there were extenuating circumstances for Virgil Van Dijk was harshly sent off early in the game by the zealous Craig Thomson for a last man challenge. With 11 men, Celtic might have achieved at least a draw, but it was a sore blow, for it was not long after Aberdeen had beaten Celtic in the Scottish Cup.

There were six draws, three of them after the League had been already sown up. The most thrilling of these was the game at Celtic Park on 2 November 2013. Stuart Armstrong had scored for Dundee United and the Tannadice men were looking strong until the very last minute of the game when Charlie Mulgrew rose to head home a Georgios Samaras cross. Other draws were at Inverness in the early part of the season, at Easter Road in October, at Motherwell and St Johnstone late in the season when things did not really matter, and a game against Ross County at Celtic Park on the Saturday after the League was won.

Foreign imports Teemu Pukki and Derk Boerrigter singularly failed to fire, and the top scorer was Kris Commons with 27 goals – and he was not generally regarded as an out and out striker. He was an attack-minded midfielder who could occasionally score a few goals. He did have a great season, however, as did Scott Brown and Joe Ledley. Stefan Johansen and Leigh Griffiths joined us in the January window, and promising youngsters like Liam Henderson and Dylan McGeouch had the occasional game, while Georgios Samaras continued to delight and exasperate in turns.

The League was won by an astonishing 29 points over Motherwell (Celtic reached 99 points and Motherwell 70!) and was wrapped up one midweek night as early as 26 March at Firhill when Celtic beat lowly Partick Thistle 5–1 with seven games remaining, and the trophy was duly presented at the end of the season after a victory over Dundee United. It was rather like the reverse of some seasons in the past. Celtic have been accused of "taking their eye off the ball" in League games as their attention was centred on other things, particularly European matters. This time it was the other way round. The League was won with very few mistakes, whereas the performances in other competitions was woeful.

Although they finished in third position in the League, there was at least a hint or two that Aberdeen might be emerging from their prolonged slumber. It was the first full season of Derek McInnes as manager. He was a tough, feisty character who had played for Rangers, and had managed St Johnstone before getting the Pittodrie job. He did bring a certain toughness to the Dons and they actually could score goals against Celtic. Indeed, they put Celtic out of the Scottish Cup in February at Celtic Park on a day when Celtic at last woke up to the idea that someone might challenge them, and of course the Dons then went on to win the Scottish League Cup, admittedly on a penalty shoot-out after an unimpressive 120 minutes of open play against Inverness Caledonian Thistle. It was the first piece of silverware seen in the Granite City for the best part of 20 years.

It was a difficult, possibly even a disastrous season for Edinburgh. Hearts, so often accused of doing the same as Rangers as far as their supporters were concerned by singing unpleasant songs, now followed Rangers at boardroom level as well and found themselves in administration. For this they were deducted 15 points and found themselves at the bottom of the League, but relegation might have happened anyway. Hibs, themselves no strangers to financial problems, managed to get to the play-off stage for a return to the top tier but blew up in a spectacularly painful fashion to Hamilton Academical on penalties.

This League title was probably the easiest of the 49. The form of the team was by no means brilliant – and this made clear by the comments of supporters on blogs and websites – but Celtic were clearly well ahead of anything else in Scotland. It would not be quite so easy in the next two seasons when Aberdeen put up a fight (they certainly came closer than in 2014) but it was increasingly difficult to argue when sneering English people talked about the "one team League". There was an element of truth in all this, but it was hardly Celtic's fault that they had kept their finances in order while others hadn't, and were thus able to stay in the Scottish Premier League.

Scottish Cup Final		
St Johnstone 2 Dundee United 0	Celtic Park	17 May
Scottish League Cup Final		
Aberdeen 0 Inverness C T 0 aet	Celtic Park	16 March
(Aberdeen won 4-2 in penalties)		
English Cup Final		
Arsenal 3 Hull City 2 aet	Wembley	17 May
English League Cup Final		
Manchester City 3 Sunderland 1	Wembley	2 March
English League		
Manchester City		

CHAPTER 46

WHO IS THIS RONNIE GUY?

2014/15

It would be a fair bet to say that no one in the Celtic community knew very much about Ronnie Deila when he was appointed manager on 6 June 2014 to replace Neil Lennon, who had departed so suddenly and so inexplicably at the end of the season. The press had predictably made collective fools of themselves by stating categorically that "their sources" had told them that so and so was going to get the job, but no one went for Ronnie Deila.

Ronnie had had a successful season with a team called Stromgodset, but then again, they were not exactly a household name in Scotland either. Norwegian football generally did not enjoy any high reputation although Celtic did already have Stefan Johansen who had worked with Deila at Stromgodset. In the past there had been Norwegians like Vidar Riseth, Tommy Rogne and Harald Brattbakk, a man who could charm supporters but fail to impress them. He did nevertheless notch the second and decisive goal in the game against St Johnstone which stopped Rangers' ten-in-a-row in 1998.

The stage was thus set for a curious couple of years in Celtic's history, in which the manager won the Scottish League two seasons out of two (a 100% record which neither Willie Maley nor Jock Stein could claim to have achieved) but then he was effectively sacked. True, the record in Europe was a shocker, but the catalyst for his departure was a defeat to Rangers in a penalty shoot-out. That however, was in the future.

Deila's first games with Celtic were played not at Celtic Park but at, of all places, Murrayfield, the home of Scottish Rugby, because Celtic Park and Hampden were being deployed for the 2014 Commonwealth Games. The games at Murrayfield were European games, but Celtic Park was ready for the first home game of the League campaign on 16 August, which was a very impressive 6–1 defeat of Dundee United. It was soon obvious that there was a very strong defence at Celtic Park with Virgil Van Dijk and Jason Denayer. Van Dijk was already in place when Deila arrived, but Denayer was on loan from Manchester City. A feature of the League campaign would be the very few goals conceded by the Celtic defence. Only Dundee United scored more than one goal against them, and that was on midwinter's day when Denayer wasn't playing!

Ronnie Deila.

Up front there was John Guidetti. Also on loan from Manchester City, the Swede became immediately popular with the Celtic crowd because his name lent itself to a rhyme along the lines of "he fairly finds the nettie" and then the illogical "he's got two good feet and the Huns are deid". He did not, perhaps, become the Henrik Larsson that some thought he might become, but he certainly made an impact.

After a shaky start which included an absolute shocker to lose 0–1 to Hamilton Academical at Celtic Park, Celtic generally won their League games, not always impressively but enough to build up a lead against their main rivals Aberdeen whom they defeated on all four League occasions that year. They also managed to qualify for the knockout stages of the Europa League after an undistinguished campaign, but the year 2014 finished with a somewhat feckless 0–0 draw against Ross County at Celtic Park following their defeat at Dundee United on midwinter's day.

Eight straight League wins followed in the New Year with the pattern usually being one of solid cast iron defending but not really a huge amount of goals being scored. Then there was a sudden and fairly inexplicable loss to St Johnstone at Parkhead one Wednesday night. The team was, however, winning, and there was success in other tournaments. We went out of the Europa League to Inter Milan, but at least we put up a respectable show, and we won the Scottish League Cup and progressed in the Scottish Cup.

We were helped by Dundee United's astonishing desire to commit suicide in the January transfer window. In a move which led inevitably and inexorably to relegation and from which they have not yet recovered, Dundee United decided to asset strip in a way that baffled the pundits and their supporters who were far from impressed by the "We have to sell to survive" sort of cant that was trotted out to them. Celtic bought Gary Mackay-Steven and Stuart Armstrong from Dundee United, and they became great assets to the side. Ironically, Dundee United then played Celtic four games in a row in all three domestic competitions, and it was no great surprise that Celtic, having drawn with United in the first Scottish Cup game at Tannadice, then beat them in the other three. One of these games was the Scottish League Cup Final and Ronnie Deila had won his first Scottish trophy.

April saw seven games and the League Championship virtually won. The only fly in the ointment was Inverness Caledonian Thistle who earned a draw in Inverness on 11 April, and then created a major shock by beating Celtic in the Scottish Cup semi-final. Celtic had cause to complain about the refereeing, but, as is often the case, this was only an excuse and fingers could well have been appointed at some of the players also.

This ruined Deila's chance of a treble in his first season, but he did not have long to wait for the Scottish League Championship. A 2–1 win at Dens Park, Dundee which saw the young Kieran Tierney being brought on as a substitute was followed by a 3–0 win across the road at Tannadice Park over the now depleted Dundee United, Leigh Griffiths proving his worth to the club with a very fine hat-trick. All this meant that Celtic needed four points in four games to become the champions, and effectively they did it on the very pleasant evening of Friday, 1

May when Dundee were the visitors.

Celtic chose this game to turn on their best performance of the season. Kris Commons scored a penalty, Scott Brown, Leigh Griffiths and James Forrest all had good goals, but the pick of them all was that of Nir Bitton, a fine player, but never exactly known for his goalscoring abilities. Until tonight, that is, when he picked up a ball about halfway inside the Dundee half. No one challenged him, so he simply hammered the ball home giving goalkeeper Scott Bain no chance.

This made it 5–0, and Celtic, although theoretically capable of being caught by Aberdeen, were, more or less, the champions. In the event Aberdeen went down 0–1 at Tannadice to Dundee United the following day, and Ronnie Deila had won the Premier League in his first season. Appropriately and fittingly, trophy presentation day at the end of the season saw a good 5–0 score over Inverness Caledonian Thistle, the team which had given Celtic so much grief not only this season but in some previous years as well. Inverness were simply swept aside by a Celtic team who showed their supporters how they should have played in the Scottish Cup semi-final

Supporters were not at this stage sure about Ronnie Deila, but it is difficult to argue against the League Championship and the League Cup. He had also introduced the "Ronnie Roar" whereby at the end of a game he walked over to the support and punched the air three times with his left hand while the supporters roared their approval.

Deservedly, Stefan Johansen was voted Player of the Year by the SPFA. It was his first full season for the club, and everyone was pleased for the way in which he had dominated midfield, teaming up well with Scott Brown. It had been a good season, and everyone looked forward to the next season, hoping in particular for a good run in Europe to add to the Scottish success.

Scottish Cup Final		
Inverness CT 2 Falkirk 1	Hampden	30 May
Scottish League Cup Final		
Celtic 2 Dundee United 0	Hampden	15 March
English Cup Final		
Arsenal 4 Aston Villa 0	Wembley	30 May
English League Cup Final		
Chelsea 2 Tottenham Hotspur 0	Wembley	1 March
English League Champions		
Chelsea		

CHAPTER 47

THE LEAGUE WINNER HAS TO GO

2015/16

2015/16 was a strange season for Celtic. Seldom, if ever, can there have been a time when supporters were so unhappy, when attendances dropped (visibly to such an extent that half the upper tier of the Lisbon Lions stands contained banners with things like "Celtic – A Team Like No Other" rather than supporters), websites and fanzines were full of critical comments, the manager was "sacked" (possibly not as brutally as in other circumstances), all these things happened, and yet the team won the Scottish Premier League!

Nor was it any thrilling, heart-attack inducing last-minute stuff. The League was won on the third last game, and the final day saw a slaughter in the sunshine as Celtic put seven goals past Motherwell, all scored by seven different players (including Jack Aitchison, who beat Davie McLean's record, which had stood for nearly 110 years, of being Celtic's youngest ever goalscorer) – and yet the manager, cheered to the echo that day, was now on his way out.

What was the reason for this mystifying state of affairs? The man at the centre of all this was the manager, Norwegian Ronnie Deila. Although the League campaign was not without its hiccups – in fact, of the seven-in-a-row since 2012,

Craig Gordon.

2016 was the one that came closest to collapsing – it is probably true to say that it was the performances in the other competitions that did for poor Ronnie. The European Champions League campaign was an embarrassing defeat to Malmo of Sweden, then the Europa League section saw Celtic finish up last. For a club whose supporters celebrated in the 67th minute about great Celtic successes in the past, this simply would not do.

The Scottish Cup and Scottish League Cup saw failure at the semi-final stage. In the League Cup we exited to Ross County. The early sending off of Efe Ambrose was harsh, but that did not excuse the rest of the performance which included a missed penalty. In the Scottish Cup, we went out to Rangers on a penalty shoot-out, always a painful way to go, but we should never have allowed it to get that length.

Particularly unpopular among the fans was John Collins, Deila's assistant. This was curious, for Collins had always been well liked as a player, but a lot seemed to stem from the decision to substitute Kris Commons in a Europa League game in the Norwegian rain against Molde. Commons was well liked by the support, and he did seem to have been harshly treated that night. And then Deila had hard luck with several players. Stefan Johansen, who had been very good the year before, seemed to lose form and even motivation to play for Celtic. That could never have been said about the ever likeable Scott Brown, but Broonie suffered a bad injury and was out for a large part of the middle of the season. Virgil Van Dijk went off to Southampton early in the season, and Jason Denayer disappeared almost as quickly as he had arrived, and they were not really adequately replaced.

The League campaign itself contained a mixture of the good and the bad. We managed to lose twice to Aberdeen at Pittodrie, an early defeat to the Dons in September indicating that a challenge was imminent. We put them in their place at Parkhead, however. There were a great deal of games ending up in draws which should have been wins, and the turn of the year was a particularly depressing time. Out of Europe, Celtic then managed to lose at home to Motherwell on 19 December, then on Boxing Day, they were winning at Tynecastle before conceding a goal at the very end. None of this was conducive to a Happy New Year, and a crowd, given at 46,067 but looking a lot less than that, saw a miserable New Year game against Partick Thistle, enlivened only by a Leigh Griffiths goal.

A mini crisis developed as January gave way to February. On Wednesday, 3 February, immediately after the exit from the Scottish League Cup at the hands of Ross County, Celtic went up to Aberdeen and lost a high-profile televised game which did indeed show the world that, for the first time for several years, there was going to be a title race. The Aberdeen supporters had banners saying things like "We're coming to get you", and it would have to be admitted, on the evidence of that game, that this was not unlikely.

Both teams now wobbled. Celtic, playing in insipid lime green, and playing in a way that reflected the strips, threw away a lead to draw at Douglas Park one Friday night against a Hamilton Accies team whom they had beaten 8–1 a few weeks ago. Then, on the following Tuesday night, the Celtic players richly deserved the boos that they received from the 41,000 crowd for a 0–0 draw against Dundee. But Aberdeen could not really take advantage of Celtic's poor performances, and were themselves prodigal of dropping points, losing to Inverness and drawing with St Johnstone.

But the day that really gave Celtic a decisive advantage was on Saturday, 19 March and it was an interesting example of the power of television. Celtic were playing a lunchtime kick-off at Rugby Park, Kilmarnock. Frankly, they were playing very badly in the pleasant spring sunshine and the large Celtic crowd behind the goal was becoming restive as Kilmarnock, having a bad season and closer to relegation than what they would have liked, were holding out until, in the very last minute of the 90, Tom Rogic picked up a ball, did the proverbial turning on a sixpence and shot home from about 25 yards.

If the effect on the Celtic community was great, then imagine what it was like in the streets of Aberdeen, where supporters were watching the pub TV on their way to their own game while their players watched in their lounge at Pittodrie. The impact of that goal on them was devastating, and it was no coincidence that the Dons went out and blew up spectacularly to lose at home to Motherwell. That made the lead four points, Celtic had a game in hand and a vastly superior goal difference, but one wonders whether Aberdeen would have lost to Motherwell if they had kicked off at the same time as Celtic.

From then on, Celtic never lost another game until the League was won. They drew again with Dundee and Ross County, teams who had given them more than a little bother this season, but crucially beat Hearts twice home and away with a comfortable 3–1 margin in each case. The League was won against Aberdeen themselves on Sunday, 8 May at a slightly more crowded Celtic Park than had been the case earlier in the season. Celtic won 3–2, although a draw would have been enough, scoring three goals before Aberdeen came back later in the game but never enough to imperil Celtic's 47th League Championship. Two of the goals were in the first half by the very successful Patrick Roberts, one of Deila's more impressive loan deals.

By this time, everyone knew that Ronnie Deila was on his way out. The statement that he was leaving at the end of the season came immediately after the penalty shoot-out defeat to Rangers, but he would be allowed to finish off the season. He did just that by winning the Scottish League, and he was much applauded for doing so, even by those who had been most vocal in wanting his departure.

One wonders what history will make of Ronnie. He lacked the quiet, gentlemanly dignity of Brendan Rodgers, and although he was not as passionate as Neil Lennon or Gordon Strachan, he did at least give us "the Ronnie Roar". He never got the luck that he perhaps deserved – and his players certainly let him down in three semi-finals - and it would be nice to see how he would get on with another British club, if the chance ever arises.

The club appointed Brendan Rodgers fairly soon after the end of the season, and there was a feeling of euphoria throughout the summer, not in any way impaired by the victory of Hibs over Rangers in the Scottish Cup Final. With three ex-Celtic players in the Hibs team – Dylan McGeouch, Anthony Stokes and Liam Henderson – it was almost like another Celtic Scottish Cup victory!

Scottish Cup Final		
Hibs 3 Rangers 2	Hampden	21 May
Scottish League Cup Final		
Ross County 2 Hibs 1	Hampden	13 March
English Cup Final		
Manchester United 2 Crystal Palace 1 aet	Wembley	21 May
English League Cup Final		
Man City 1 Liverpool 1	Wembley	28 February
(Manchester City won 3–1 on penalties)		
English League		
Leicester City		

CHAPTER 48

BRENDAN THE BOLD

2016/17

There was an element of upstaging, one felt, in the timing of the announcement of Brendan Rodgers as the new manager in May 2016, in that it came about the same time as the Rangers v. Hibs Scottish Cup Final and inevitably drew some attention from it. It was immediately felt that Celtic had made a good choice, and the atmosphere around Parkhead was not dissimilar to that of summer 2000 when Martin O'Neill had been appointed.

Brendan Rodgers had been manager of Swansea City and Liverpool. As manager of Liverpool he had been very unlucky to lose the English League in 2014 when the team unaccountably made mistakes – including a hideous one from Steve Gerard against Chelsea, and then the loss of three goals in about 10 minutes to Crystal Palace – and Liverpool lost form at exactly the wrong time. He was not employed at the time that Celtic approached him. He accepted without a great deal of persuasion, for he was a Celtic supporter and knew how good the club could become. He also knew what the club meant to so many people.

It has to be stressed that the club was NOT in any sort of crisis. They were League Champions with many fine players, and Rodgers was very careful not to throw the baby out with the bathwater (as happened with some other clubs when a new manager was appointed) by putting on the transfer list all those whom the previous regime had cherished. He did, however, make a few signings – notably

Celtic celebrate the League triumph at Tynecastle on 2 April 2017.

Scott Sinclair and Moussa Dembele – and they would make a fairly immediate impact.

His first game was a defeat in Gibraltar, but that was soon put right and by the time that the Scottish League season began, Celtic were making progress in Europe. The League season opened with a solid and gratifying, if unspectacular, win at Tynecastle and by the end of August two further wins had been registered – a good one at McDiarmid Park, and then Aberdeen inexorably obeyed their own self-imposed rule that no matter how well they are doing elsewhere, they must lose at Celtic Park. Griffiths, Forrest, Sinclair and Rogic scored the goals in the 4–1 defeat of the Dons and Celtic Park was happy.

But if that was good, what happened next on 10 September was even better. Rangers came to Celtic Park, but in every sense this was a new Rangers. Rangers used to come to Celtic Park bristling with arrogance, supremacy, Protestantism and "we are the people" triumphalism. This lot came expecting a thrashing and left, having got one. Moussa Dembele, who had already made his mark at Celtic Park, scored a hat-trick, and Scott Sinclair and Stuart Armstrong notched the others in a game which set down a marker for the rest of the season. Rangers indeed never did recover, and the tenure of manager Mr Warburton, a likeable but totally out of his depth Englishman, was now living on borrowed time.

Celtic then dropped a point up at Inverness on 18 September to a late and definitely preventable equaliser but that was the last loss of points that the team suffered until long after the winter shutdown. A few teams put up a brave fight – Dundee at Dens Park, Aberdeen at Pittodrie both held Celtic to 1–0, for example – but the best game for a spectator to watch, without a doubt was the game at Fir Park, Motherwell on 3 December, which Celtic won 4–3 after having been 0–2 and then 2–3 down!

There were a further seven games in December. It is often said that League Championships are won in December when loads of League games are played, the pitches aren't always so good and the overseas players are struggling to deal with the cold and darkness of a Scottish December. But Celtic won them all, beating Hamilton Accies (twice), Dundee, Partick Thistle and Ross County and finishing with the 2–1 win at Ibrox which guaranteed a Happy New Year. It also meant that Celtic started again in late January after the midwinter break some 19 points ahead of Rangers, and with a game in hand! The goalscorers were Dembele and Sinclair. It had not been such a Merry Christmas for the fast-developing Callum McGregor, for he had been sent off on Christmas Eve at Hamilton by referee Willie Collum for a reason that the TV commentators (let alone the Celtic fans) found hard to explain.

2016 had been, by any standards a good year for the club. Celtic had already won the Scottish League Cup and performed reasonably well in Europe, if we ignore a naïve defensive performance at the Nou Camp and a bad defeat at home to Borussia Monchengladbach. Two games against Manchester City had produced honourable draws. So many young players were developing under Brendan Rodgers – Kieran Tierney, Callum McGregor, Patrick Roberts, Moussa Dembele – that it was hard not to feel optimistic about the future.

The consistent good form continued as the football resumed. St Johnstone, Hearts, Aberdeen and then St Johnstone again were all beaten and progress was made in the Scottish Cup as well. There were even some moments of comedy. One concerned a free kick outside the box at Inverness on Wednesday, 1 March. Stuart Armstrong stood poised to take it, but he was delayed by at least a minute as the referee Andrew Dallas tried to sort out all the pushing and shoving by defenders and attackers as they all tried to jostle for position. In spite of the referee's best efforts, they were still all at it as Stuart took the free-kick. But it mattered not a whit, because the free-kick bypassed them all and went into the net!

The other piece of humour concerned the Scottish press. On 12 March, Celtic dropped their second point of the season when Rangers earned a draw at Celtic Park with a late equaliser. To be fair, the game was an even one and Rangers probably deserved their point, but the press immediately went into overdrive praising Rangers excessively for their "character" and "quality" in such a way that one would have thought they had won the European Cup! Rangers possibly believed it as well, but reality returned about six week later when Celtic put them out of the Scottish Cup!

By that time, Celtic were League Champions. They beat Dundee 2–1 at Dens Park on 19 March which allowed them to become champions at Tynecastle on 2 April with eight Scottish League games left to play! Scott Sinclair put Celtic 2–0 up before half-time, and the second half was simply a rout. Stuart Armstrong and Patrick Roberts scored brilliant goals and then Scott Sinclair got his hat-trick by converting a penalty kick. Then came the celebrations at a virtually empty stadium apart from the small section of ground allocated to the delirious Celtic fans.

In the remaining eight games, they managed to draw another two times – to Partick Thistle on the Wednesday night immediately after the League was

Scottish Cup Final		
Celtic 2 Aberdeen 1	Hampden	27 May
Scottish League Cup Final		
Celtic 3 Aberdeen 0	Hampden	27 November
English Cup Final		
Arsenal 2 Chelsea 1	Wembley	27 May
English League Cup Final		
Manchester City 3 Southampton 2	Wembley	26 February
English League		
Chelsea		

won, and then to Ross County in a game which saw Scott Brown sent off after a disgraceful piece of amateur dramatics by a County player. 29 April, the first day after the "split", saw Celtic at Ibrox, and Rangers might have hoped for a little consolation for what had been a desolate season for them. Rightly Celtic did not spare them and hammered them 5–1 with almost embarrassing ease.

The other games were won well and the defeat of Hearts at Celtic Park on the last day of the League season (after which the trophy was duly presented) meant that Celtic had gone the whole season unbeaten and with only four draws. There remained only the Scottish Cup Final against Aberdeen. It was a good game but Celtic were always on top and the late goal scored by Tom Rogic, the Wizard of Oz, meant that Celtic did indeed deserve in 2017 the name "the Invincibles".

The phrase "Happy Days" did not quite cover it!

CHAPTER 49

THE DOUBLE TREBLE

2017/18

Season 2017/18 was the season that Celtic repeated their feat of 2016/17. It was called the "Double Treble" and was unprecedented in Scottish footballing history. Celtic had almost done it in 1970, and Rangers in 1994 but each had fallen down in the Scottish Cup Final. Celtic's win in that competition a few weeks after they had won the League meant that they had now achieved this feat, and that Brendan Rodgers had been with Celtic for two years and had yet to lose a competition. As in 2016/17 Celtic had beaten Aberdeen in both domestic cups, so in 2017/18 Motherwell had been the victims on both days.

It was not quite as good a season as the previous one. There were quite a few draws at home, and four defeats, the most important of which was the 0–4 defeat by Hearts at Tynecastle the week before Christmas which finally brought to an end the unbeaten run which had lasted 69 games. Another was at Rugby Park, Kilmarnock in early February on the somewhat controversial artificial surface (but that was no real excuse) and the other two were at the end of the season. But at no point could it honestly be said that Celtic were seriously challenged. If there had been a serious challenger, it might have

Mikael Lustig, Tom Rogic and Kieran Tierney show off the silverware.

been a different story. As it was, Aberdeen might have challenged but kept losing to Celtic – and even Rangers!

A depressing side of the season had been the poor performance, yet again, in Europe. True, Celtic were in a very difficult section but the performances against Paris Saint Germain, particularly the one at Parkhead, and Bayern Munich were embarrassing in the extreme. True, there was one excellent result in beating Anderlecht in Belgium, which showed what could be done, and that was enough to qualify Celtic for the last 32 of the Europa League, but that too ended in a disgraceful defeat to Zenit St Petersburg after a reasonable performance in the first leg at Celtic Park.

The Scottish Premier League season started in August with a 4–1 defeat of Hearts at Celtic Park, and then a couple of good away wins at Partick Thistle and Kilmarnock, before a slightly disappointing failure to beat St Johnstone at Parkhead. It would be the start of a trend to lose games at home that we should have won, but credit to St Johnstone for a gritty performance. Indeed, it might have been a defeat but for Callum McGregor's late strike.

The first game against Rangers this season was at Ibrox, and it was a rather embarrassingly easy victory with two second-half goals from Tom Rogic and Leigh Griffiths, and the feeling that even if Rangers had managed to pull one back, Celtic would have been able to up a gear or two. Celtic, however, could have done with upping a gear in the home game against Hibs at the end of September, for the general consensus was the Neil Lennon's Hibs side were the better team. Once again Callum McGregor was Celtic's goalscorer (twice), but Hibs looked sharper and deserved their draw. Possibly for the first time this season, we began to hear the word "jaded" in the context of Celtic.

Two games at the end of October typified Celtic's season. On Wednesday, 25 October, they defeated Aberdeen 3–0 at Pittodrie, a performance which even had Pittodrie legend Willie Miller using words like "outstanding". Kieran Tierney scored once and Moussa Dembele twice and it was indeed a very impressive performance. But then to the chagrin of their fans, three days later at Celtic Park they could only draw 1–1 with Kilmarnock. This pattern of winning the games that they had to – against Aberdeen and Rangers away from home, but failing to finish off some apparently lesser teams at Celtic Park was definitely a feature of the season.

Late November saw the League Cup triumph over Motherwell and then we played Motherwell again the next two games – a spirited draw at Fir Park in midweek, and then the game in which Odsonne Edouard made his mark – a 5–1 beating of the Claret and Ambers at Celtic Park. The game which saw the end of the 69-unbeaten run came at Tynecastle on 17 December. The severity of the defeat was a surprise, but it had been hinted at the week before at Easter Road when, although Celtic got a 2–2 draw, once again the impression was that Hibs were the better side who really should have won, and would have done so but for Mikael Lustig's clearance in that mad ending to the game. But Aberdeen were beaten once again – 3–0 a couple of days before Christmas, and 2017 ended with a goalless draw against Rangers at Parkhead.

This was disappointing, and once again we heard the clichés about "jaded" and "tired" and so on, and even more depressingly we even heard some Celtic players being booed by an ungrateful minority of the support. And yet, Celtic were still nine points ahead of the field!

Rumours were prevalent about the imminent transfer of Moussa Dembele, who did indeed look lethargic and uninterested, so lethargic and uninterested, in fact, that no serious offer was made for him! There was apparently, an £18 million bid from Brighton, which, one suspects, the media made up, but in any case, after the midwinter shutdown, Moussa took a tumble to himself and by the end of January the damage done by the Edinburgh clubs before Christmas was put right with two good wins over Hearts and Hibs at Celtic Park.

The defeat at Kilmarnock and a dreadful goalless draw against St Johnstone did not matter so much as the wins at Pittodrie and Ibrox – once again we see the ability to win the games that they really had to. The Ibrox one was a classic, particularly as the Rangers support (they of all people really ought to have known better!) decided to believe the press that they were bound to beat Celtic and open up the League race. They were given a boost when a linesman (a Conservative MP, by total coincidence, of course!) shouted "Red card! Red card!" to get Jozo Simunovic dismissed, but Celtic still won 3–2 with goals from Rogic, Dembele and Edouard.

Effectively, this ended things, as Celtic now meandered to the title. The draw at Motherwell was a hard-fought one, but the one against Dundee at Celtic Park was a boring shocker. A sort of soap opera began to develop about the post-split fixtures. For one thing, they should have been published a great deal earlier but apparently there was an issue of whether Rangers should come to Celtic Park on the first day after the split when the League could be won. "Oh, we cannae hae that" they said and Celtic were put to Easter Road to win the League there. Sadly, Celtic wearing their awful pink strip failed to co-operate and lost 1–2, so it was Celtic Park against Rangers after all that the League was won!

And how! 5–0 was a travesty, for it should have been a whole lot more. The pick of the goals were a couple scored just before half-time by Edouard and Forrest, Mikael Lustig wore a policeman's hat, and half-time saw some Rangers supporters depart the scene. It was a total rout, and given that Celtic had defeated them 4–0 in the Scottish Cup a fortnight earlier, it was hard to resist the conclusion that this was the biggest gulf between the two clubs that there had ever been.

Celtic then lived up to their reputation of this season of not winning games that did not matter, and Aberdeen registered a very rare (almost a collector's item) win at Celtic Park on the day that the trophy was presented. Forty-nine times the Scottish League, and the following week came the Scottish Cup Final. Now, that was a game that Celtic did have to win – and they duly did so – 2–0 v. Motherwell and the Double Treble. Life was sweet!

It was a great time to be a Celtic supporter. All that was really required now was for the team to raise their game and put up some sort of performance in Europe. Apart from anything else, it would silence all these know-alls trying to tell us how easy it all was in Scotland!

Scottish Cup Final		
Celtic 2 Motherwell 0	Hampden	19 May
Scottish League Cup Final		
Celtic 2 Motherwell 0	Hampden	26 November
English Cup Final		
Chelsea 1 Manchester United 0	Wembley	19 May
English League Cup Final		
Manchester City 3 Arsenal 0	Wembley	25 February
English League		
Manchester City		

9781781562932

#0004 - 040918 - C14 - 234/156/14 - PB - 9781781562932